THE VISUAL MAESTRO'S HANDBOOK

Mastering Modern Video Editing

Yatendra Kumar Singh 'Manuh'

CONTENTS

INTRODUCTION

The Visual Maestro's Handbook: Mastering Modern Video Editing

Unlock the powerful secrets of professional video editing and take your creative projects to the next level with *The Visual Maestro's Handbook*. Whether you're an aspiring filmmaker, a seasoned editor, or a content creator, this comprehensive guide will transform the way you craft videos.

What's Inside:

- **Chapter 1: Laying the Foundation**: Dive into the basics of video editing, from understanding key terms and software to setting up your editing workspace.

- **Chapter 2: Advanced Cutting Techniques**: Master the art of precise cuts, seamless transitions, and effective storytelling through editing.

- **Chapter 3: Sound Design and Audio Editing**: Elevate your video projects with high-quality audio that enhances the viewer's experience.

- **Chapter 4: Special Effects and Visual Enhancements**: Learn how to add dazzling effects and sophisticated animations to captivate your audience.

- **Chapter 5: Color Correction and Grading**: Achieve professional-grade color correction and grading to ensure your videos look polished and consistent.

- **Chapter 6: Adding Text and Graphics**: Discover the techniques for creating engaging titles, lower thirds, and motion graphics.

- **Chapter 7: Exporting and Sharing Your Video**: Find the best practices for exporting your videos with optimal settings for various platforms.

- **Chapter 8: Trends and Innovations in Video Editing**: Stay ahead of the curve with insights into AI, VR, 360-degree video, and cloud-based collaboration.

- **Chapter 9: Special Project: Creating a Short Film**: Follow a step-by-step guide to plan, shoot, and edit your very own short film.

- **Chapter 10: Future-Proofing Your Skills**: Learn how to stay relevant in the ever-evolving world of video editing with tips on continuous learning and emerging trends.

Why You'll Love This Book:

- **Expert Insights**: Written by industry professionals with years of experience in video editing and filmmaking.

- **Practical Examples**: Includes step-by-step tutorials and real-world examples to apply what you learn immediately.

- **Creative Inspiration**: Packed with tips and tricks to spark your creativity and make your projects stand out.

- **Comprehensive Coverage**: Covers all aspects of video editing, from basics to advanced techniques and the latest trends.

Whether you're creating content for social media, working on a personal project, or producing professional videos, *The Visual Maestro's Handbook* is your ultimate guide to mastering modern video editing. Transform your vision into reality and become a visual maestro today!

◆ ◆ ◆

CHAPTER 1: INTRODUCTION TO VIDEO EDITING

Historical Evolution of Video Editing: From Film to Digital

Video editing has undergone a remarkable transformation over the past century, evolving from labor-intensive manual techniques to highly sophisticated digital processes. Understanding this historical evolution provides a vital context for appreciating today's advanced video editing tools and practices. Here's a detailed look at the journey:

1. Early Beginnings: The Birth of Film Editing

- **Silent Film Era (1890s-1920s)**: In the early days, film editing was a rudimentary craft. Editors manually cut and spliced film strips using a magnifying glass and a splicer. This painstaking process required precision and a keen eye for detail.

2. The Golden Age of Hollywood (1930s-1950s)

- **Linear Editing**: With the advent of sound in films, editing became more complex. Editors sequenced scenes linearly, physically moving strips of film through machines. The Moviola editing machine, invented in 1924, became a standard tool, allowing editors to view and cut film strips more efficiently.

3. The Rise of Television and Video Tape (1950s-1970s)

- **Introduction of Video Tape Editing**: The 1950s saw the

development of video tape recording (VTR) technology. Video tape editing was initially performed in a linear fashion, similar to film. However, the transition to electronic editing introduced time-based editing systems, allowing for greater flexibility.

4. The Digital Revolution (1980s-2000s)

- **Non-Linear Editing Systems (NLEs):** The late 1980s and early 1990s marked a turning point with the advent of non-linear editing systems. These systems, such as Avid Media Composer (1989) and Adobe Premiere (1991), allowed editors to access any frame of the video without requiring sequential playthrough. This innovation drastically improved efficiency and creative freedom.

- **Transition from Analog to Digital Media:** The shift from analog to digital formats facilitated smoother transitions, better quality, and easier duplication. Digital video files replaced celluloid film and magnetic tape, enabling more sophisticated editing techniques and effects.

5. The Age of Accessible Editing (2000s-Present)

- **Proliferation of Consumer Editing Software:** The 2000s saw video editing software becoming accessible to a wider audience, with programs like Final Cut Pro and iMovie catering to both professionals and amateurs. This democratization of video editing fostered a new generation of creators.

- **Advancements in Technology:** High-definition (HD) and ultra-high-definition (UHD/4K) formats have become standard. Cloud-based editing and real-time collaboration tools further revolutionized the industry, making it easier for teams to work remotely.

6. The Future of Video Editing: Emerging Trends

- **Artificial Intelligence (AI) and Automation:** AI-powered tools are now assisting editors by automating repetitive tasks, suggesting edits, and even creating video content autonomously.

- **Virtual and Augmented Reality (VR/AR)**: Cutting-edge VR and AR technologies are opening new frontiers in immersive video editing, offering viewers interactive and immersive experiences.
- **Collaborative Editing and Cloud Solutions**: Cloud-based platforms enable collaborative editing, where multiple editors can work on the same project from different locations, streamlining the editing process.

Significance of Video Editing in Contemporary Media

Video editing plays a crucial role in the contemporary media landscape, shaping how stories are told and consumed across various platforms. Here's a breakdown of its significance:

1. Enhancing Storytelling

- **Bringing Vision to Life**: Editors transform raw footage into coherent narratives, ensuring that the director's vision is realized. The choice of cuts, transitions, and pacing can significantly impact the mood and message of a story.
- **Creating Emotional Impact**: Effective editing can evoke emotions, build tension, and create suspense. By carefully selecting shots and orchestrating sequences, editors control the emotional journey of the audience.

2. Increasing Engagement

- **Capturing Attention**: In an era of content overload, compelling video editing ensures that videos stand out and capture viewers' attention. Techniques like dynamic cuts, engaging graphics, and strategic use of music can keep audiences hooked.
- **Retention and Rewatchability**: Well-edited videos are more likely to be watched to the end and revisited. Quality editing enhances viewer experience, making the

content more memorable and impactful.

3. Enhancing Communication

- **Clear and Concise Messaging**: Editing helps distill complex information into understandable and engaging formats. Educational videos, documentaries, and corporate communications rely heavily on effective editing to convey their messages clearly.

- **Visual Storytelling**: By using visual cues, motion graphics, and effects, editors can enhance the storytelling process, making it more engaging and accessible.

4. Facilitating Creativity and Innovation

- **Pushing Artistic Boundaries**: Video editing software provides tools for creativity, allowing editors to experiment with visual effects, timelines, and multimedia elements. This fosters innovation in how stories can be told and experienced.

- **Collaboration and Shared Vision**: Modern editing platforms facilitate collaboration among creators, enabling multiple inputs and perspectives. This collaborative process enriches the creative outcome and aligns it with the collective vision.

5. Supporting Marketing and Branding

- **Brand Consistency**: Editing ensures that marketing videos adhere to brand guidelines, maintaining visual and thematic consistency across all content. This is vital for building brand identity and recognition.

- **Converting Viewers to Customers**: Engaging and persuasive video content is a powerful tool in marketing strategies. Through effective editing, brands can create compelling narratives that resonate with their target audience, driving engagement and conversions.

6. Empowering Independent Creators

- **Access to Tools and Platforms**: The accessibility of affordable editing software and online platforms empowers independent creators. This democratization of video editing allows for diverse voices and stories to be shared with the world.
- **Monetization Opportunities**: Edited video content can be monetized through platforms like YouTube, Twitch, and TikTok, providing income opportunities for content creators. High-quality editing can lead to increased viewership and engagement, enhancing revenue potential.

7. Shaping Public Perception and Culture

- **Influencing Opinions**: Through documentaries, news, and social media, video editing shapes public perception and discourse. Editorial choices—what to include or exclude, how to frame a story—can have significant cultural and political implications.
- **Reflecting and Driving Trends**: Trends in video editing often reflect broader cultural shifts and technological advancements. Editors not only respond to current trends but also drive the evolution of media aesthetics and standards.

Basic Terminology in Video Editing

Understanding basic terminology is essential for anyone starting their journey in video editing. Here are some key terms you'll frequently encounter:

1. Clip: A small segment of video or film that forms part of a larger project. Think of clips as the building blocks of your final video.

2. Timeline: The workspace where clips, audio, and effects are arranged sequentially in a video editing software. It's a visual representation of your project from start to finish.

3. Transition: A method of moving from one clip to another. Common transitions include cuts (direct switch between clips), fades (gradual change from one clip to another), and wipes (one clip is replaced by another through a specific movement).

4. Cut: The most basic form of transition, where one shot is immediately followed by another. It's often used to maintain pace or to guide the viewer's attention.

5. Split: Dividing a single clip into two or more separate clips. This allows editors to apply different effects or transitions to each segment.

6. Trim: Removing unwanted sections from the beginning or end of a clip. This often involves cutting out unneeded parts to ensure the final video flows smoothly.

7. Sequence: A series of clips arranged in a specific order to form a portion of your project. Sequences can be edited and refined independently before being integrated into the main timeline.

8. Frame Rate: The number of individual frames displayed per second in a video. Common frame rates include 24 fps (frames per second) for films, 30 fps for television, and 60 fps for high-motion content.

9. Aspect Ratio: The width-to-height ratio of the video frame. Standard aspect ratios include 4:3 (traditional television), 16:9 (widescreen), and 21:9 (cinematic).

10. Resolution: The amount of detail in a video, typically measured in pixels (e.g., 1920x1080 for Full HD, 3840x2160 for 4K). Higher resolutions result in clearer and more detailed images.

11. Codec: A software or hardware component that compresses and decompresses digital video. Popular codecs include H.264, HEVC (H.265), and ProRes.

12. Keyframe: A point in your timeline where a change occurs. Keyframes are used in animation and effects to signal the start and end of transformations like movement or opacity.

13. B-Roll: Supplemental footage that is intercut with the main shot (A-Roll) to add context or visual interest. B-Roll footage often includes cutaway shots, establishing shots, or relevant action shots.

14. Color Correction: The process of altering or enhancing the color of video footage to achieve a natural and consistent appearance. This ensures that colors look correct and balanced across the entire project.

15. Color Grading: The creative process of modifying and enhancing the color and mood of video footage. Color grading can give a specific look or style to your video, such as a vintage feel or a dramatic tone.

16. Render: The process of creating the final video file from the edited project. Rendering involves processing all clips, effects, and transitions to produce a complete video.

17. LUT (Look-Up Table): A pre-defined color lookup table used to apply specific color grading settings. LUTs are often used to achieve a consistent look or to match the color grading of different shots.

18. Audio Sync: Ensuring that the audio aligns perfectly with the corresponding video footage. Audio sync is essential for dialogues, interviews, and music videos.

19. Workflow: The planned sequence of operations or processes in video editing. Efficient workflow helps achieve better productivity and ensures a smooth editing process.

20. Proxy: Lower-resolution versions of video files used during editing to improve performance. Once editing is complete, the project can be rendered using the original high-resolution files.

Software and Equipment Essentials

Starting a journey in video editing requires both the right software and equipment. Here's an overview of the essentials you need:

A. Editing Software

Choosing the right video editing software is crucial for your workflow and final output. Here are some popular options:

    1. **Adobe Premiere Pro**

- **Overview**: Industry-standard software widely used by professionals. Offers comprehensive tools for video editing, color correction, and audio mixing.
- **Pros**: Extensive features, regular updates, and integration with other Adobe products.
- **Cons**: Subscription-based model, which can be costly.

2. **Final Cut Pro**

- **Overview**: A powerful editing program exclusive to Mac users. Known for its speed, efficiency, and advanced features.
- **Pros**: Optimized for Mac hardware, seamless performance, and a one-time purchase cost.
- **Cons**: Mac-only, so not suitable for PC users.

3. **DaVinci Resolve**

- **Overview**: A professional-grade video editor that excels in color grading and visual effects.
- **Pros**: Free version available with robust features, highly regarded for color correction.
- **Cons**: Steeper learning curve compared to other software.

4. **iMovie**

- **Overview**: User-friendly and free software for Mac users, suitable for beginners.
- **Pros**: Simple interface, easy to learn, and comes pre-installed on Macs.
- **Cons**: Limited advanced features compared to professional software.

5. **Sony Vegas Pro**

- **Overview**: A versatile editing software known for its flexibility and professional features.
- **Pros**: User-friendly interface, good for both beginners and professionals.

- **Cons**: Less support and updates compared to other leading software.

B. Essential Equipment

Having the right hardware setup is vital for efficient and high-quality video editing:

1. **Computer**

   - **Processor (CPU)**: A powerful CPU ensures smooth editing and rendering. Look for multi-core processors like Intel Core i7/i9 or AMD Ryzen 7/9.

   - **RAM**: More RAM enables better performance, especially for handling large files. Aim for at least 16GB, with 32GB or more for professional work.

   - **Graphics Card (GPU)**: A dedicated GPU like NVIDIA GeForce RTX or AMD Radeon provides better performance for rendering and effects.

   - **Storage**: SSDs (Solid State Drives) are faster than HDDs (Hard Disk Drives) and improve overall system speed. Consider a combination of SSD for operating system and software, and HDD for storing files.

2. **Monitors**

   - **Resolution and Color Accuracy**: A high-resolution monitor (4K) and good color accuracy are essential for detailed editing and color grading.

   - **Dual Monitor Setup**: Having two monitors can significantly enhance your workflow by allowing more screen real estate for timeline and preview windows.

3. **External Hard Drives**

   - **Backup and Storage**: Regular backups are crucial to avoid data loss. External drives with large capacities (1TB or more) and fast transfer speeds are ideal.

4. **Headphones and Speakers**

   - **Audio Editing**: Quality headphones and speakers are

necessary for accurate audio mixing and sound editing. Look for headphones with flat frequency response to get an accurate representation of your audio.

5. **Input Devices**

- **Keyboard and Mouse**: Programmable keyboards and ergonomic mice can increase efficiency and reduce strain during long editing sessions.
- **Drawing Tablets**: Useful for precise editing and working with motion graphics and visual effects.

6. **Camera and Accessories**

- **Quality Footage**: A good camera is essential for capturing high-quality footage. DSLR or mirrorless cameras are popular among creators.
- **Tripods and Stabilizers**: Help maintain steady shots and improve the overall quality of your footage.
- **Lighting**: Proper lighting setups can dramatically enhance the look of your video. Consider investing in softboxes, LED panels, and ring lights.

Whether you're a budding editor or looking to upgrade your current setup, having the right software and equipment can make a significant difference in your video editing journey.

CHAPTER 2: UNDERSTANDING VIDEO FORMATS AND CODECS

Choosing the correct video format is essential for ensuring compatibility, quality, and performance across different devices and platforms. Here's an overview of some of the most common video formats:

1. MP4 (MPEG-4 Part 14)

- **Overview**: The most widely used format for video files. It provides excellent compression and quality, making it ideal for online streaming.
- **Benefits**: High compression efficiency, broad compatibility, and excellent quality-to-size ratio.
- **Use Cases**: Streaming on YouTube, social media, and most devices.

2. MOV (QuickTime File Format)

- **Overview**: Developed by Apple, this format is known for its high quality and is widely used in professional video editing.
- **Benefits**: High-quality video and audio, versatile with both lossy and lossless compression.
- **Use Cases**: Editing in Final Cut Pro, archiving high-quality footage, and professional projects.

3. AVI (Audio Video Interleave)

- **Overview**: One of the oldest video formats, developed by Microsoft. It offers good quality but can result in larger file sizes.
- **Benefits**: High-quality video and extensive compatibility with Windows software.
- **Use Cases**: Archival storage, legacy projects, and applications that require uncompressed video.

4. MKV (Matroska Video Format)

- **Overview**: An open-source format that can hold an unlimited number of video, audio, and subtitle tracks in one file.
- **Benefits**: Highly flexible and capable of containing a vast amount of data types.
- **Use Cases**: High-definition video content, movies, and TV shows with multiple language tracks or subtitles.

5. AVCHD (Advanced Video Coding High Definition)

- **Overview**: Developed for high-definition video cameras, this format provides excellent quality and compression for HD recordings.
- **Benefits**: High-quality video with efficient storage, ideal for HD and Full HD video.
- **Use Cases**: HD camcorders, Blu-ray discs, and professional video recording.

6. FLV (Flash Video)

- **Overview**: Originally developed by Adobe, this format was widely used for streaming video on the internet.
- **Benefits**: Small file sizes and compatibility with Adobe Flash Player.
- **Use Cases**: Legacy web video content and Flash applications.

7. WMV (Windows Media Video)

- **Overview**: Developed by Microsoft, this format is known for its efficient compression and good quality.
- **Benefits**: Small file sizes with decent quality, compatible with Windows platforms.
- **Use Cases**: Streaming on Windows-based platforms and applications.

8. WEBM

- **Overview**: An open, royalty-free format designed for web use. It offers good quality with efficient compression.
- **Benefits**: Open format with high-quality playback on web browsers and devices.
- **Use Cases**: HTML5 video, web streaming, and web applications.

9. MPEG (Moving Picture Experts Group)

- **Overview**: A family of standards used for coding audio-visual information. MPEG-2 and MPEG-4 are the most common variations.
- **Benefits**: High-quality video and audio, with efficient compression ratios.
- **Use Cases**: Television broadcast, DVD video, and online streaming.

10. HEVC (High Efficiency Video Coding / H.265)

- **Overview**: The successor to H.264, this format offers significantly better compression and quality.
- **Benefits**: Superior quality at lower bitrates, ideal for high-resolution video.
- **Use Cases**: 4K UHD video streaming, high-quality video content, and modern video applications.

Each of these formats has its strengths and ideal use cases, depending on your specific needs and project requirements. Choosing the right format ensures your video is compatible with your desired platforms and delivers the best quality possible. If you'd like to learn more about any specific format or move on to another topic, just let me know!

Introduction to Codecs (H.264, ProRes, DNxHD, etc.)

In video editing, codecs are essential tools that compress and decompress digital video files. Understanding the most commonly used codecs will help you choose the right one for your projects. Here's a detailed introduction:

1. H.264 (MPEG-4 AVC)

- **Overview**: One of the most widely used codecs today, known for its high compression efficiency without sacrificing too much quality.
- **Benefits**: Provides excellent quality-to-size ratio, making it ideal for streaming and sharing online.
- **Use Cases**: Streaming on YouTube, Vimeo, and other online platforms; recording on consumer cameras; and general-purpose editing.

2. ProRes

- **Overview**: A codec developed by Apple, known for high-quality performance and optimized for professional-grade editing.
- **Benefits**: Maintains high image quality with efficient editing and playback, particularly on Apple devices.
- **Use Cases**: Professional video production, post-production workflows, and high-quality archival storage.

3. DNxHD (Digital Nonlinear Extensible High Definition)

- **Overview**: Developed by Avid, this codec is designed for high-quality HD video editing and post-production.
- **Benefits**: Offers robust image quality and seamless integration with Avid editing systems.
- **Use Cases**: Broadcast production, professional editing,

and mastering for distribution.

4. HEVC (H.265)

- **Overview**: The successor to H.264, offering significantly better compression rates and improved quality.
- **Benefits**: Delivers high-quality video at lower bitrates, making it ideal for 4K and UHD content.
- **Use Cases**: 4K UHD video streaming, high-quality video storage, and modern video applications.

5. VP9

- **Overview**: An open-source codec developed by Google, known for its high efficiency and support for higher resolutions.
- **Benefits**: Provides excellent compression and quality, especially for web streaming.
- **Use Cases**: Streaming on platforms like YouTube and Google Chrome, web applications, and HTML5 video.

6. XAVC

- **Overview**: A codec developed by Sony, designed for recording and playback of high-resolution video.
- **Benefits**: Supports 4K and HD resolutions with high-quality performance.
- **Use Cases**: Professional video production, camera recording, and high-definition broadcasting.

7. XVID

- **Overview**: An open-source codec based on the MPEG-4 standard, popular for its versatility and compatibility.
- **Benefits**: Offers good compression and quality, widely supported on various platforms and devices.
- **Use Cases**: DVD ripping, online video distribution, and general-purpose video playback.

8. CineForm

- **Overview**: A high-performance codec developed by

GoPro, known for its lossless compression.
- **Benefits**: Provides excellent image quality with real-time editing performance.
- **Use Cases**: Professional video editing, VR content production, and high-quality archiving.

Comparison Chart:

Codec	Compression Efficiency	Image Quality	File Size	Usage Scenarios
H.264	High	Good	Medium	Online streaming, consumer video
ProRes	Medium	High	Large	Professional editing, archival storage
DNxHD	Medium	High	Large	Broadcast, professional editing
HEVC	Very High	Excellent	Small	4K streaming, UHD content
VP9	High	Good	Medium	YouTube streaming, web applications
XAVC	Medium	High	Large	High-definition broadcasting, camera recording
XVID	High	Good	Medium	DVD ripping, online distribution
CineForm	Low	Excellent	Large	Professional editing, VR content

Understanding these codecs will help you make informed decisions about which to use for different stages of your video editing process, ensuring optimal quality and efficiency. If you're interested in diving deeper into any of these codecs or exploring another topic, feel free to ask! ◆◆

Choosing the Right Format and Codec for Projects

Selecting the right format and codec for your video projects is crucial for achieving the desired quality, compatibility, and performance. Here's a guide to help you make the best choice for different types of projects:

1. Online Streaming
- **Ideal Formats**: MP4, WEBM

- **Preferred Codecs**: H.264, VP9
- **Why**: These formats and codecs offer high compression efficiency and flexibility, making them perfect for streaming platforms like YouTube and Vimeo. They provide a good balance between quality and file size, ensuring smooth playback across different devices and internet speeds.

2. Professional Editing and Post-Production

- **Ideal Formats**: MOV, MXF
- **Preferred Codecs**: ProRes, DNxHD, CineForm
- **Why**: Professional codecs such as ProRes and DNxHD maintain high image quality and are optimized for editing workflows. MOV and MXF formats are widely adopted in professional environments due to their high fidelity and compatibility with editing software like Final Cut Pro and Avid Media Composer.

3. High-Resolution and 4K Content

- **Ideal Formats**: MP4, MOV, MXF
- **Preferred Codecs**: HEVC (H.265), XAVC
- **Why**: HEVC provides superior compression for high-resolution content, reducing file sizes while maintaining excellent quality. XAVC is designed for 4K and HD recording, ensuring high-quality performance suitable for professional use.

4. Archival and Mastering

- **Ideal Formats**: MOV, MKV
- **Preferred Codecs**: ProRes, DNxHD, CineForm
- **Why**: For archival purposes, it's essential to use codecs that retain maximum quality. Formats like MOV and MKV support high-quality codecs, ensuring that the master files are preserved with minimal loss of detail.

5. Social Media

- **Ideal Formats**: MP4, WEBM
- **Preferred Codecs**: H.264, VP9
- **Why**: Social media platforms often require specific formats and codecs to ensure compatibility. H.264 in MP4 format is widely supported and provides efficient compression. VP9 in WEBM format is also a good choice for certain platforms, offering good quality for online videos.

6. DVDs and Blu-Ray Discs

- **Ideal Formats**: MPEG-2, AVCHD, MP4
- **Preferred Codecs**: MPEG-2, H.264
- **Why**: For physical media like DVDs and Blu-Rays, MPEG-2 and AVCHD are standard due to their compatibility and quality. H.264 is also used for Blu-Ray discs, offering efficient compression and high-quality output.

Factors to Consider When Choosing a Format and Codec:

- **Compatibility**: Ensure that the chosen format and codec are compatible with the platforms and devices where your video will be viewed.
- **Quality**: Consider the level of detail and clarity required for your project. Professional projects often demand higher quality codecs.
- **File Size**: Balancing quality and file size is crucial, especially for online streaming and sharing.
- **Editing Workflow**: Select codecs that integrate smoothly with your editing software and workflow, especially for professional editing.
- **Future-Proofing**: Choose formats and codecs that are likely to remain relevant and supported, ensuring longevity for your projects.

By understanding the strengths and ideal use cases of different formats and codecs, you can make informed decisions that enhance the quality and efficiency of your video projects. Feel free to ask if you want to delve deeper into any of these topics or explore another area! ��

Converting and Compressing Video Files

Converting and compressing video files are essential skills in video editing, ensuring compatibility, reducing file sizes, and optimizing performance. Here's a comprehensive guide on how to convert and compress video files effectively:

1. Converting Video Files:

A. Understanding Conversion:

- **Purpose**: Converting video files changes the format or codec to ensure compatibility with different devices, platforms, or editing software.
- **Common Scenarios**: Converting a high-resolution file to a smaller format for sharing, changing from one codec to another for editing, or converting to meet platform-specific requirements.

B. Conversion Tools:

- **HandBrake**: An open-source tool that supports numerous formats and codecs. Ideal for converting videos for various devices and purposes.
- **Adobe Media Encoder**: Part of the Adobe Creative Cloud suite, it provides advanced options for converting and compressing video files.
- **FFmpeg**: A powerful command-line tool for video conversion, known for its flexibility and extensive format support.
- **VLC Media Player**: Beyond being a media player, VLC offers basic video conversion functionality for popular formats.

C. Conversion Process:

1. **Import the Video**: Open your chosen conversion

software and import the video file you wish to convert.

2. **Choose the Output Format**: Select the desired output format and codec. Ensure it matches the target platform's requirements.

3. **Adjust Settings**: Configure resolution, bitrate, frame rate, and other settings as needed. This step allows for fine-tuning the quality and size.

4. **Start Conversion**: Initiate the conversion process. The software will encode the video into the new format.

2. Compressing Video Files:

A. Understanding Compression:

- **Purpose**: Compression reduces the file size of videos, making them easier to store, upload, and share without significantly compromising quality.

- **Types of Compression**:
  - ○ **Lossless Compression**: Reduces file size without losing any quality, retaining all original data.
  - ○ **Lossy Compression**: Reduces file size by removing some data, resulting in a smaller file with slight quality degradation.

B. Compression Tools:

- **HandBrake**: Also effective for compression, offering presets for different output requirements.

- **Adobe Media Encoder**: Provides advanced compression settings suitable for various professional needs.

- **FFmpeg**: Offers command-line options for precise control over compression parameters.

C. Compression Process:

1. **Import the Video**: Load the video file into your compression tool.

2. **Select Output Settings**: Choose the appropriate output format and codec. H.264 is a common choice for

more) provide ample screen real estate, making it easier to manage multiple timelines and windows.

3. Peripherals

- **Keyboard and Mouse**: Ergonomic and programmable keyboards and mice can improve editing efficiency. Look for devices with customizable keys and functions.

- **Drawing Tablets**: Useful for precision tasks like motion graphics and visual effects. Brands like Wacom offer high-quality drawing tablets compatible with video editing software.

- **Audio Equipment**: Quality headphones and studio monitors are essential for accurate audio editing and mixing. Brands like Sennheiser and Audio-Technica offer reliable options.

4. External Storage and Backup Solutions

- **External Hard Drives**: High-capacity external drives (1TB or more) with fast transfer speeds (USB 3.1/3.2 or Thunderbolt) are crucial for backing up and transferring large files.

- **NAS (Network Attached Storage)**: A NAS system provides scalable and redundant storage solutions, ideal for professional environments with large amounts of data.

- **Cloud Storage**: Services like Google Drive, Dropbox, and Adobe Creative Cloud offer convenient backup and collaboration options.

5. Cooling and Power

- **Cooling Systems**: Effective cooling solutions, such as liquid cooling or high-performance air coolers, keep your system running smoothly under heavy workloads.

- **Uninterruptible Power Supply (UPS)**: A UPS protects your workstation from power outages and surges, ensuring no data loss during crucial editing sessions.

6. Additional Considerations

- **Software Optimization**: Ensure your editing software is optimized for your hardware. Keep drivers and software updated to leverage the latest performance improvements.
- **Workspace Setup**: Organize your workstation ergonomically. Invest in a comfortable chair, an adjustable desk, and proper lighting to reduce strain during long editing sessions.

Having the right hardware setup will greatly enhance your editing capabilities and overall efficiency, enabling you to handle complex projects with ease.

Choosing the Right Software (Adobe Premiere Pro, Final Cut Pro, DaVinci Resolve, etc.)

Selecting the right video editing software is a critical step in optimizing your workflow and achieving professional results. Here's a detailed look at some of the top video editing software options available in 2025:

1. Adobe Premiere Pro

- **Overview**: An industry-standard editing software used by professionals worldwide. It offers extensive features for video editing, color correction, audio mixing, and more.
- **Pros**:
  - Comprehensive toolset suitable for all levels of editing
  - Seamless integration with other Adobe Creative Cloud apps like After Effects and Photoshop
  - Regular updates and a strong community support network
- **Cons**:
  - Subscription-based model can be costly over

time

- Requires a powerful computer for optimal performance

2. Final Cut Pro

- **Overview**: A professional-grade video editing software from Apple, exclusive to macOS. Known for its speed, efficiency, and advanced editing features.
- **Pros**:
  - Optimized for Mac hardware, providing smooth and efficient performance
  - One-time purchase, no ongoing subscription fees
  - Innovative features like magnetic timeline, multicam editing, and advanced color grading tools
- **Cons**:
  - Mac-only software, not available for Windows users
  - Learning curve for those new to the Mac ecosystem

3. DaVinci Resolve

- **Overview**: A powerful video editing, color grading, and post-production software. Widely recognized for its advanced color correction capabilities.
- **Pros**:
  - Comprehensive free version with robust features
  - Industry-leading color grading tools
  - Integrated Fusion for VFX and Fairlight for advanced audio post-production
- **Cons**:
  - Steeper learning curve compared to other

      editors

- Can be resource-intensive, requiring powerful hardware for optimal performance

4. iMovie

- **Overview**: A user-friendly editing software from Apple, ideal for beginners and casual editors. Provides essential editing tools with an intuitive interface.

- **Pros**:
  - Free and pre-installed on Mac devices
  - Simple and easy to learn, great for quick edits and basic projects
  - Integration with other Apple applications and devices

- **Cons**:
  - Limited advanced features compared to professional-grade software
  - Mac-exclusive, not available on Windows

5. Sony Vegas Pro

- **Overview**: A versatile video editing software known for its user-friendly interface and powerful features. Suitable for both beginners and professionals.

- **Pros**:
  - Flexible and customizable workflow
  - Good balance of features for editing, audio mixing, and special effects
  - One-time purchase, no subscription required

- **Cons**:
  - Less frequent updates and support compared to leading software
  - Mid-tier performance for high-end professional use

6. HitFilm Pro

- **Overview**: A video editing and visual effects software that combines editing, compositing, and VFX tools in one package.
- **Pros**:
  - Strong emphasis on visual effects and compositing
  - Affordable pricing with a range of features
  - Good community and support resources
- **Cons**:
  - Can be overwhelming for beginners due to the abundance of features
  - Performance may lag behind top-tier software in some scenarios

When choosing the right video editing software, consider the following factors:

- **Project Requirements**: Identify the complexity and scope of your projects. Professional-grade software is suited for complex and high-quality projects, while simpler tools may suffice for basic edits.
- **Platform Compatibility**: Ensure the software aligns with your operating system and hardware.
- **Budget**: Balance the features and costs. Subscription models offer regular updates, while one-time purchases may be more budget-friendly in the long run.
- **Learning Curve**: Consider your experience level and willingness to learn new tools. User-friendly software might be better for beginners, while advanced tools offer more creative control for experienced editors.
- **Community and Support**: Access to tutorials, forums, and customer support can significantly impact your learning and troubleshooting experience.

Each software has its strengths and weaknesses, and the best choice depends on your specific needs and preferences.

Organizing Project Files and Workspaces

Efficient organization of project files and workspaces is crucial for a smooth and productive video editing process. Here's a comprehensive guide on how to set up your files and workspace effectively:

1. Organizing Project Files

A. Create a Standardized Folder Structure:

- **Project Folder**: Start by creating a main folder for your project. Inside this folder, create subfolders for specific types of files. A standardized structure makes it easier to locate and manage your assets.
  - **Footage**: Store all raw video clips. Consider organizing by date, scene, or camera angle.
  - **Audio**: Separate folders for dialogue, sound effects, background music, and other audio elements.
  - **Graphics**: Include titles, lower thirds, motion graphics, and any other visual elements.
  - **Projects**: Save project files and sequences here. This keeps your editing software files organized.
  - **Exports**: Keep final exported videos and version iterations in a dedicated folder.
  - **Documents**: Store scripts, storyboards, and other project-related documents.
  - **Backup**: Regular backups of important files to ensure nothing is lost.

Example Folder Structure:

```
Project_Name/
|
├── Footage/
|   ├── Scene_01/
|   └── Scene_02/
|
```

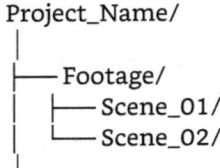

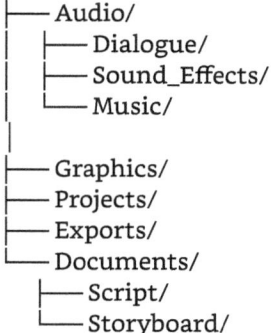

```
├── Audio/
│   ├── Dialogue/
│   ├── Sound_Effects/
│   └── Music/
│
├── Graphics/
├── Projects/
├── Exports/
└── Documents/
    ├── Script/
    └── Storyboard/
```

B. Naming Conventions:

- **Consistent Naming**: Use clear and consistent naming conventions for all files. This ensures all team members can easily understand and locate files.

- **Version Control**: Include version numbers or dates in file names (e.g., "Scene_01_Clip_v1.mov" or "Project_Final_20250126.prproj"). This helps track edits and updates.

C. Metadata and Tagging:

- **Use Metadata**: Add metadata and tags to your files for easier searching and organization. Most editing software allows you to tag clips with keywords, descriptions, and other metadata.

D. Backups and Redundancy:

- **Regular Backups**: Schedule regular backups to external drives or cloud storage to avoid data loss.

- **Redundancy**: Use multiple backup methods (local, external, cloud) to ensure data integrity.

2. Setting Up Your Workspace

A. Customizing the Interface:

- **Workspace Layout**: Most editing software allows customization of the workspace layout. Arrange panels and toolbars to suit your workflow.

- **Save Layout Presets**: Save custom layouts as presets for different types of projects (e.g., editing, color correction, audio mixing).

B. Optimizing Performance:

- **Cache and Media Settings**: Set up efficient cache and media storage settings to enhance performance. Store cache files on fast SSDs or NVMe drives.

- **Proxy Editing**: Use proxy files (lower-resolution versions of your video) for smoother editing, especially with high-resolution footage.

C. Keyboard Shortcuts:

- **Custom Shortcuts**: Customize keyboard shortcuts to speed up your workflow. Learn and use shortcuts for common tasks to save time.

- **Shortcut Command Boards**: Consider using programmable keyboards or command boards with customizable keys for quick access to tools and functions.

D. Multitasking and Organization:

- **Dual Monitors**: Use dual monitors to extend your workspace, placing the timeline on one screen and the playback window on another.

- **Task Management**: Maintain a task list or project management tool to track progress and deadlines. Tools like Trello, Asana, or even a simple spreadsheet can be helpful.

E. Environment and Ergonomics:

- **Comfortable Setup**: Invest in a comfortable chair, desk, and lighting to reduce strain during long editing sessions.

- **Cable Management**: Organize and manage cables to keep your workspace clutter-free and efficient.

F. Collaboration and Sharing:

- **Cloud Collaboration**: Use cloud-based editing tools

and platforms for real-time collaboration with team members. Services like Adobe Creative Cloud or Frame.io enable seamless collaborative workflows.

- **Sharing Settings**: Ensure your sharing settings are configured for secure and efficient file sharing with team members and clients.

By carefully organizing your project files and optimizing your workspace, you can create an efficient and productive video editing environment. This organization not only saves time but also reduces stress, allowing you to focus on the creative aspects of your work.

CHAPTER 3: SETTING UP YOUR WORKSTATION

Tips for Efficient Workflow

Maintaining an efficient workflow in video editing can greatly enhance productivity and ensure high-quality results. Here are some essential tips to streamline your process:

1. Plan and Organize Before You Start

- **Storyboarding**: Create a storyboard or shot list to visualize your project. This helps you plan your edits and understand the sequence of shots.
- **Script Breakdown**: Annotate your script with notes on specific shots, transitions, and effects you plan to use.

2. Use Proxy Editing for High-Resolution Footage

- **Create Proxies**: Use lower-resolution proxy files for editing, especially if working with 4K or higher resolution footage. This improves performance and makes editing smoother.
- **Switch Back to Original**: Once editing is complete, switch back to the original high-resolution footage for final rendering.

3. Master Keyboard Shortcuts Custom Shortcuts: Learn and utilize keyboard shortcuts for common tasks (e.g., cutting, trimming, applying effects) to speed up your workflow.

- **Programmable Keyboards**: Consider using

programmable keyboards or command boards to create custom shortcuts and macros.

4. Create and Use Templates

- **Project Templates**: Set up project templates with pre-configured settings and folder structures. This saves time and ensures consistency across projects.
- **Effect Presets**: Save frequently used effects, transitions, and color grading settings as presets for quick application.

5. Maintain an Organized Timeline

- **Label and Color Code**: Use labels and color codes to categorize different types of clips (e.g., dialogue, B-roll, graphics) on your timeline.
- **Nest Sequences**: Organize complex projects by nesting sequences. This helps keep your main timeline clean and easier to manage.

6. Regularly Save and Backup Projects

- **Auto-Save**: Enable auto-save features in your editing software to prevent data loss.
- **Manual Backups**: Regularly create manual backups of your project files to external drives or cloud storage.

7. Optimize Your System Performance

- **Manage Cache Files**: Regularly clear cache files to free up system resources and maintain performance.
- **Update Software**: Keep your editing software and hardware drivers up to date to benefit from performance improvements and new features.

8. Leverage Multi-Camera Editing

- **Sync Multi-Camera Clips**: Use the multi-camera editing feature for projects shot with multiple cameras. This allows you to switch between angles seamlessly during editing.

- **Organize Multicam Footage**: Label and group all multicam clips to avoid confusion and streamline the editing process.

9. Collaborate Efficiently

- **Use Collaborative Tools**: Utilize cloud-based collaboration tools like Frame.io, Adobe Team Projects, or Google Drive to share files and receive feedback in real-time.
- **Track Changes**: Keep track of changes and revisions made by collaborators to maintain consistency.

10. Regularly Review and Refine Your Workflow

- **Assess Workflow**: Periodically review your workflow and identify areas for improvement. Make adjustments based on new techniques or software features.
- **Stay Updated**: Keep up with industry trends and updates in editing software to continuously enhance your skills and workflow efficiency.

Implementing these tips can help you achieve a more efficient and productive video editing process, allowing you to focus on creativity and quality.

CHAPTER 4: BASIC EDITING TECHNIQUES

Importing and Organizing Footage

Mastering the basics of importing and organizing your footage is crucial for a smooth and efficient video editing process. Here's a step-by-step guide to get you started:

1. Importing Footage

A. Preparing Your Media:

- **Back Up Your Footage**: Before importing, ensure you have backed up your footage to prevent any data loss.

- **Verify Formats**: Check that all your footage formats are compatible with your editing software. Convert any incompatible formats using reliable conversion tools if necessary.

B. Importing into Editing Software:

1. **Open Your Project**: Launch your editing software (e.g., Adobe Premiere Pro, Final Cut Pro, DaVinci Resolve) and open your project or start a new one.

2. **Importing Media**:
   - **Manual Import**: Go to the 'File' menu, select 'Import' or 'Import Media,' and navigate to the folders where your footage is stored.
   - **Drag and Drop**: Drag your media files directly from your file explorer into the project's media bin or library within the software.

3. **Organize Upon Import**:

- ◦ **Folders and Bins**: Create folders or bins within your project to categorize different types of footage (e.g., A-roll, B-roll, interviews).
- ◦ **Label and Tag**: Label your clips with relevant names and add tags or markers for easy identification.

2. Organizing Footage

A. Creating a Logical Folder Structure:

- • **Project Folder**: Establish a main folder for your project. Within this folder, create subfolders for each type of content, such as:
  - ◦ **Raw Footage**: Store all original video clips here.
  - ◦ **Audio**: Separate folders for dialogue, background music, sound effects.
  - ◦ **Graphics**: Titles, lower thirds, motion graphics, still images.
  - ◦ **Sequences**: Store different editing sequences or timelines.
  - ◦ **Exports**: Final renditions and versioned exports.
  - ◦ **Documents**: Scripts, storyboards, shot lists, notes.

Example Folder Structure:

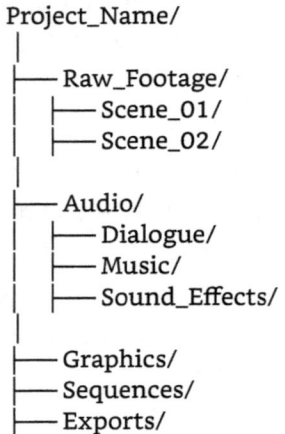

```
Project_Name/
│
├── Raw_Footage/
│   ├── Scene_01/
│   ├── Scene_02/
│
├── Audio/
│   ├── Dialogue/
│   ├── Music/
│   ├── Sound_Effects/
│
├── Graphics/
├── Sequences/
├── Exports/
```

```
└── Documents/
    ├── Scripts/
    └── Storyboards/
```

B. Naming Conventions:

- **Consistent Naming**: Use clear and consistent naming conventions for all files. This helps you and your team easily locate specific clips and assets.
- **Version Control**: Include version numbers or dates in file names (e.g., "Scene_01_take_01.mov" or "Interview_v2_01_26_2025.mp4").

C. Using Metadata and Tags:

- **Add Metadata**: Utilize the metadata features in your editing software to add keywords, comments, and other relevant information to your clips.
- **Apply Tags**: Tag your clips with descriptors like "B-roll," "interview," "action scene," which can help you quickly filter and find footage during editing.

D. Organizing Within the Software:

- **Bins/Folders**: Use bins or folders within your editing software to categorize your clips. This mirrors the folder structure in your file system.
- **Label with Colors**: Many editing programs allow you to color-code your clips. Use this feature to visually distinguish between types of footage or different stages of the editing process.

E. Reviewing and Logging Footage:

- **Watch and Log**: Review all imported footage to become familiar with the content. Log important details about each clip, including in and out points, significant moments, and any issues.
- **Create Subclips**: Create subclips from longer footage to isolate specific moments or scenes. This helps streamline the editing process and keeps your project organized.

By importing and organizing your footage effectively, you'll save time and reduce stress during the editing process. This foundational step ensures a smooth transition to the more creative aspects of video editing.

Timeline and Sequence Basics

Understanding the basics of timelines and sequences is essential for effective video editing. Here's a comprehensive guide to get you started:

1. Timelines

A. What is a Timeline?

- **Definition**: The timeline in video editing software is a visual representation of your project's progress from start to finish. It helps you organize and arrange your clips, audio, effects, and transitions in a sequential order.
- **Tracks**: The timeline consists of multiple tracks that can hold video, audio, and additional elements like text or graphics. Tracks are typically layered, with the topmost track being the most visible or audible.
  - **Video Tracks**: Hold video clips, images, and other visual elements.
  - **Audio Tracks**: Contain audio clips such as dialogue, music, and sound effects.
  - **Additional Tracks**: Some software allows for dedicated tracks for text, effects, and markers.

B. Navigating the Timeline:

- **Playhead**: Indicates the current frame being displayed in the preview window. You can move the playhead to different points in the timeline to edit or review your project.
- **Zoom In/Out**: Zoom in for precise edits or zoom out to see the entire sequence. This allows better control over timing and spacing.

- **Scrubbing**: Moving the playhead manually to scan through the footage. This helps you find specific moments or frames in your project.

C. Basic Timeline Operations:

- **Cutting and Trimming**: Use tools like the razor tool to cut clips into segments. Trim the beginning or end of clips to remove unwanted sections.
- **Ripple and Roll Edits**: Adjust the timing of clips without leaving gaps. Ripple edit moves all subsequent clips, while roll edit adjusts the in and out points of adjacent clips.
- **Drag and Drop**: Add clips to the timeline by dragging and dropping them from the media bin. Rearrange clips by dragging them to different positions on the timeline.
- **Snapping**: Enable snapping to align clips precisely. This ensures clips start and end exactly where you want them.

2. Sequences

A. What is a Sequence?

- **Definition**: A sequence is a specific section of your project composed of organized clips, audio, and effects. Sequences can be edited individually and later assembled into a final project.
- **Multiple Sequences**: You can create and manage multiple sequences within the same project, each representing different scenes, parts, or versions.

B. Creating and Managing Sequences:

- **New Sequence**: Create a new sequence by specifying its settings, such as resolution, frame rate, and audio configuration.
- **Sequence Presets**: Many editing software provide presets for different types of projects. Choose a preset that matches your project's requirements (e.g., YouTube,

4K, 1080p).

- **Renaming and Organizing**: Name your sequences clearly to keep track of them easily. Organize sequences in bins or folders within the project panel.

C. Nesting Sequences:

- **Nested Sequences**: Embed one sequence within another to streamline complex projects. This allows you to treat multiple clips as a single unit, making it easier to apply effects and transitions.
- **Benefits**: Nesting reduces clutter on the timeline, simplifies editing, and helps with organization and efficiency.

D. Editing Within Sequences:

- **Cut and Trim**: Perform detailed edits within individual sequences. This allows you to refine specific sections before integrating them into the main project.
- **Apply Effects**: Add effects, transitions, and color grading to sequences. This helps maintain a consistent look and feel across different sections.

3. Best Practices

A. Consistent Workflow: Develop a consistent workflow for managing timelines and sequences. This helps streamline the editing process and ensures you don't miss any important steps.

B. Organize Your Tracks: Keep related clips and audio organized in specific tracks. For example, use one track for main footage, another for B-roll, and separate tracks for audio elements. **C. Regularly Save Your Progress**: Save your project frequently to prevent data loss. Consider enabling auto-save features in your editing software.

By mastering the basics of timelines and sequences, you'll be able to manage your projects more effectively and create polished, professional videos.

Cutting, Trimming, and Splitting Clips

Mastering cutting, trimming, and splitting clips is fundamental to creating smooth and engaging video content. Here's a detailed guide on these essential techniques:

1. Cutting Clips

A. Understanding Cutting:

- **Definition**: Cutting involves removing unwanted sections from your clips or dividing one clip into multiple segments.
- **Purpose**: It allows you to refine your footage by eliminating unnecessary parts and organizing your project effectively.

B. Tools and Methods:

- **Razor Tool**: Most video editing software includes a razor or blade tool to cut clips at specific points on the timeline.
- **Keyboard Shortcuts**: Learn shortcuts for cutting to speed up the editing process. For example, in Adobe Premiere Pro, the shortcut is "C" for the razor tool and "Ctrl+K" or "Cmd+K" for cutting at the playhead.
- **Clip Context Menu**: Right-click on a clip and select "Cut" from the menu for a quick cut at the desired point.

C. Steps to Cut Clips:

1. **Select the Razor Tool**: Click the razor tool in your editing software or use the keyboard shortcut.
2. **Position the Playhead**: Move the playhead to the exact frame where you want to make the cut.
3. **Make the Cut**: Click on the clip at the playhead position to cut it into two segments.
4. **Repeat**: Repeat the process to make multiple cuts as needed.

2. Trimming Clips

A. Understanding Trimming:

- **Definition**: Trimming adjusts the in and out points of a clip to remove unwanted sections from the beginning or end.
- **Purpose**: It helps fine-tune the timing of your clips, ensuring a smooth and precise edit.

B. Tools and Methods:

- **Trim Tool**: Use the trim tool in your editing software to adjust the in or out points of a clip.
- **Ripple Edit Tool**: This tool allows you to trim a clip while automatically closing gaps created by the trim. The ripple edit tool ensures that the rest of the timeline moves to accommodate the trim.
- **Keyboard Shortcuts**: Shortcuts for trimming can vary by software. For example, in Premiere Pro, you can use the "Q" and "W" keys for ripple trimming.

C. Steps to Trim Clips:

1. **Select the Trim Tool**: Click the trim tool or use the appropriate shortcut.
2. **Position the Playhead**: Place the playhead at the point where you want to trim.
3. **Adjust In/Out Points**: Click and drag the edge of the clip inward or outward to trim the beginning or end.
4. **Apply Ripple Edit**: If using the ripple edit tool, the subsequent clips will automatically adjust to fill the gap.

3. Splitting Clips

A. Understanding Splitting:

- **Definition**: Splitting divides a single clip into two or more separate clips at a specified point on the timeline.
- **Purpose**: It allows for more precise edits and the application of different effects or transitions to

individual segments.

B. Tools and Methods:

- **Blade Tool**: Use the blade tool (also known as the razor tool) to split clips.
- **Keyboard Shortcuts**: Like cutting, many editing software have specific shortcuts for splitting clips, such as "Ctrl+K" or "Cmd+K" in Premiere Pro.

C. Steps to Split Clips:

1. **Select the Blade Tool**: Activate the blade tool or use the shortcut.
2. **Position the Playhead**: Move the playhead to the exact point where you want to split the clip.
3. **Make the Split**: Click on the clip at the playhead position to divide it into two separate clips.

4. Best Practices for Cutting, Trimming, and Splitting:

A. Review Your Footage: Watch your footage multiple times to identify the best points for cutting, trimming, and splitting. **B. Use Markers**: Place markers on the timeline to remember specific points or moments in your footage. **C. Preview Edits**: Always preview your timeline after making cuts, trims, or splits to ensure the edits appear seamless. **D. Undo Mistakes**: Use the undo feature if you make a mistake. Most editing software allows you to revert to previous actions easily.

By mastering these techniques, you'll be able to create polished and professional videos, ensuring that your footage is precisely edited to match your creative vision.

Working with Multiple Tracks

Effectively working with multiple tracks in your video editing software is essential for creating complex and professional-quality projects. Here's a detailed guide on how to manage and utilize multiple tracks:

1. Understanding Multiple Tracks

A. Track Types:

- **Video Tracks**: Used for visual elements such as footage, images, titles, and graphics. You can layer multiple video tracks to achieve various effects like picture-in-picture (PiP) and overlays.
- **Audio Tracks**: Used for sound elements such as dialogue, background music, sound effects, and voiceovers. Separate audio tracks allow for better control over each sound element.
- **Graphics and Text Tracks**: Some software provides dedicated tracks for text and graphics, making it easier to manage these elements.

B. Track Layers:

- **Layering**: Multiple tracks are layered in the timeline, with higher tracks obscuring lower ones. This is useful for compositing, where you can stack different visual elements on top of each other.
- **Visibility**: You can toggle the visibility of each track to focus on specific elements during editing. This is helpful for isolating certain clips or effects.

2. Adding and Managing Tracks:

A. Adding Tracks:

1. **Add Video Track**: Right-click on the timeline and select "Add Track" or "Add Video Track." You can also use shortcuts or menu options specific to your software.
2. **Add Audio Track**: Similarly, add a new audio track by right-clicking and selecting "Add Audio Track."
3. **Multiple Tracks**: Repeat the steps to add multiple video and audio tracks as needed for your project.

B. Renaming and Organizing Tracks:

- **Rename Tracks**: Right-click on the track name and select "Rename" to give it a descriptive name (e.g., "Main Footage," "Voiceover," "Background Music"). This helps keep your project organized.

- **Color-Coding**: Use color-coding to visually distinguish different tracks. Many editing software allows you to assign colors to tracks or clips.

C. Locking and Muting Tracks:

- **Lock Track**: Lock a track to prevent accidental edits. This is useful for protecting finished sections or important clips.
- **Mute Track**: Mute audio tracks to focus on specific sound elements. Muting is helpful when you want to isolate dialogue or music during editing.

3. Syncing Audio and Video Tracks:

A. Manual Syncing:

- **Align Clips**: Place the audio and video clips on separate tracks and manually align them based on visual and audio cues, such as clapperboard marks or waveform peaks.
- **Fine-Tuning**: Use audio waveform displays to fine-tune the alignment for precise syncing.

B. Automatic Syncing:

- **Sync by Timecode**: If your footage and audio have timecode metadata, use the sync-by-timecode feature available in professional editing software.
- **Sync by Audio**: Some software features automatic audio syncing that aligns video and audio tracks based on their waveforms. This is useful for multicam projects or separate audio recordings.

4. Applying Effects to Multiple Tracks:

A. Track-Based Effects:

- **Video Effects**: Apply video effects to all clips on a track by adding effects directly to the track header. This ensures a consistent look across multiple clips.

- **Audio Effects**: Apply audio effects like equalization (EQ), reverb, or compression to entire audio tracks for consistent sound across the project.

B. Nested Sequences:

- **Create Nested Sequences**: Group multiple clips into a nested sequence and apply effects to the entire sequence. This simplifies complex projects and keeps your main timeline organized.

5. Best Practices for Working with Multiple Tracks:

A. Plan Your Tracks:

- **Pre-Planning**: Determine the number of tracks and their purpose before starting your project. This helps maintain an organized timeline.
- **Reserve Tracks**: Leave empty tracks between different types of elements for flexibility and future adjustments.

B. Optimize Performance:

- **Proxy Editing**: Use proxy files for high-resolution footage to improve playback and editing performance.
- **Disable Playback of Unused Tracks**: Temporarily disable playback of tracks not in use to reduce system load.

C. Regularly Review and Clean Up:

- **Review Timeline**: Periodically review your timeline to ensure tracks are organized and free of unnecessary clips.
- **Delete Unused Tracks**: Remove empty or unused tracks to keep your project clean and manageable.

By mastering the use of multiple tracks, you can create more complex, dynamic, and professional videos. This skill allows for greater creative control and precision in your editing process.

CHAPTER 5: ADVANCED EDITING TECHNIQUES

Using Transitions and Effects

Mastering the use of transitions and effects can elevate your video projects, adding professional polish and creative flair. Here's a detailed guide to help you get started:

1. Transitions

A. Understanding Transitions:

- **Definition**: Transitions are visual effects placed between two clips to smooth the change from one shot to another.
- **Purpose**: They help convey a passage of time, change of location, or shift in mood. Common transitions include cuts, fades, wipes, and dissolves.

B. Common Types of Transitions:

- **Cut**: The most straightforward transition, where one shot is immediately followed by another. Often used for maintaining pace and flow.
- **Fade In/Fade Out**: Gradually transitions from black to a clip (fade in) or from a clip to black (fade out). Commonly used at the beginning and end of videos.
- **Dissolve**: A gradual blend from one clip to another, often used to signify the passage of time or a dream sequence.
- **Wipe**: One clip is replaced by another with a specific

motion (e.g., horizontal, vertical). Often used in related shots or dream sequences.

- **Slide**: Similar to a wipe, but the incoming clip slides in over the outgoing clip.
- **Cutaway**: An abrupt shift from the main shot to a secondary shot, often used as a B-roll.

C. Applying Transitions:

1. **Select Transition**: Browse the list of available transitions in your editing software's effects panel. Drag and drop the chosen transition onto the timeline between two clips.
2. **Adjust Duration**: Extend or shorten the transition by dragging its edges on the timeline.
3. **Fine-Tuning**: Use the transition settings panel to adjust parameters such as direction, speed, and style to fit your project's needs.

2. Effects

A. Understanding Effects:

- **Definition**: Effects are visual or audio enhancements applied to clips to alter their appearance or sound.
- **Purpose**: They help enhance storytelling, create mood, and draw viewers' attention to specific elements. Effects can be simple (e.g., brightness adjustment) or complex (e.g., adding motion graphics).

B. Common Types of Effects:

- **Color Correction**: Adjusts the color balance, brightness, and contrast to ensure a consistent look across all clips.
- **Color Grading**: Applies stylistic color effects to enhance or change the mood of the video.
- **Blur and Sharpen**: Adjusts the clarity of the image, often used for focus effects or to obscure sensitive information.

- **Distortion**: Alters the shape or perspective of the image, often used for creative or stylistic purposes.
- **Stabilization**: Reduces or eliminates camera shake, creating smoother footage.
- **Green Screen (Chroma Key)**: Replaces a specific color (usually green or blue) with another image or video, commonly used for background replacement.

C. Applying Effects:

1. **Select Effect**: Browse the effects panel in your editing software and drag the chosen effect onto the desired clip(s) on the timeline.
2. **Effect Controls**: Use the effect controls panel to adjust the parameters of the effect. This includes settings such as intensity, duration, and application areas.
3. **Keyframing**: Use keyframes to animate effects over time. Keyframing allows you to vary the intensity or parameters of an effect at specific points in the timeline.

3. Best Practices for Using Transitions and Effects

A. Subtlety is Key: Use transitions and effects sparingly to avoid overwhelming the viewer. Aim for a natural and seamless look. **B. Match the Mood**: Ensure that the chosen transitions and effects align with the overall tone and style of your project. **C. Preview and Adjust**: Always preview your work after applying transitions and effects. Make necessary adjustments to ensure they integrate smoothly with the rest of the project. **D. Use Presets**: Many editing software offers preset transitions and effects that can save time and provide professional results. Customize these presets as needed. **E. Keep It Consistent**: Maintain a consistent style throughout your project to ensure a cohesive final product.

By mastering the use of transitions and effects, you can add depth and creativity to your video projects, making them more engaging and visually appealing.

Creating Smooth Motion with Keyframing

Keyframing is a powerful technique that allows you to create smooth and precise animations within your video projects. Here's a detailed guide on how to use keyframing to achieve fluid motion:

1. Understanding Keyframes

A. Definition: Keyframes are markers that define the start and end points of any transition. They control properties such as position, opacity, scale, and rotation over time.

B. Purpose: Keyframes allow you to create animations, effects, and transitions that change gradually between keyframe points, resulting in smooth motion.

2. Basic Keyframing Techniques

A. Setting Up Keyframes:

1. **Select the Clip**: Choose the clip you want to animate in your timeline.
2. **Open Effects Controls**: Go to the effects control panel (or equivalent in your editing software).
3. **Enable Keyframing**: Click the stopwatch icon next to the property you want to animate (e.g., position, scale).

B. Adding Keyframes:

1. **First Keyframe**: Move the playhead to the starting point of the animation and set the first keyframe by adjusting the property value (e.g., move the clip to the starting position).
2. **Second Keyframe**: Move the playhead to the end point of the animation and set the second keyframe by adjusting the property value to the desired end state (e.g., move the clip to the final position).
3. **Intermediate Keyframes**: Add additional keyframes between the starting and ending points for more complex animations.

C. Adjusting Keyframes:

- **Ease In/Ease Out**: Apply easing effects to keyframes to create more natural acceleration and deceleration. Most editing software allows you to adjust keyframe interpolation.
- **Editing Keyframes**: Drag keyframes on the timeline to adjust their timing or use the keyframe graph editor for precise control over motion curves.

3. Practical Applications of Keyframing

A. Motion Paths:

1. **Position Animation**: Use keyframes to move a clip along a defined path. This is useful for animations like text fly-ins or object movements.
2. **Bezier Curves**: Adjust motion paths using Bezier curves for smooth, curved movements.

B. Scaling and Zooming:

1. **Scale Animation**: Create a zoom-in or zoom-out effect by keyframing the scale property.
2. **Dynamic Zoom**: Combine scale and position keyframes to create a dynamic zoom effect that pans across the scene.

C. Rotations:

1. **Rotate Animation**: Keyframe the rotation property to spin or tilt a clip over time.
2. **360-Degree Spins**: Achieve full rotations by setting keyframes at 0° and 360° (or multiple rotations for continuous spinning).

D. Opacity and Fades:

1. **Fade In/Fade Out**: Use keyframes to animate the opacity property, creating smooth fade-ins and fade-outs for clips or elements.
2. **Crossfades**: Apply crossfades between clips by

keyframing the opacity of overlapping clips.

E. Complex Animations:

1. **Compound Effects**: Combine multiple keyframed properties (e.g., position, scale, rotation) for intricate animations.
2. **Nested Animations**: Create nested sequences with keyframed elements to manage complex animations more efficiently.

4. Best Practices for Keyframing

A. Plan Your Animation: Sketch out your animation path and keyframe positions before you start. This helps create a clear vision and makes the keyframing process smoother. **B. Consistency**: Maintain consistent timing and motion styles throughout your project to create a cohesive look. **C. Fine-Tune Timing**: Use the timeline and graph editor to fine-tune keyframe timing and motion curves for precise control. **D. Preview Animations**: Regularly preview your animations to ensure they look smooth and natural. Make adjustments as needed. **E. Use Presets**: Many editing software offers keyframe presets for common animations. Use these as a starting point and customize them to fit your project.

By mastering keyframing techniques, you can add dynamic and professional-quality animations to your video projects, enhancing their visual appeal and storytelling.

Speed Adjustments and Slow Motion

Adjusting the speed of your video clips can add a dramatic effect, emphasize actions, or create a specific mood. Here's a detailed guide on how to make effective speed adjustments and create smooth slow-motion effects:

1. Speed Adjustments

A. Understanding Speed Adjustments:

- **Definition**: Speed adjustments involve changing the

playback speed of a video clip. You can speed up or slow down the footage to achieve different visual effects.

- **Purpose**: Speed adjustments can portray fast-paced action, slow down moments for emphasis, or synchronize footage with audio.

B. Tools and Methods:

- **Rate Stretch Tool**: Use the rate stretch tool in your editing software to adjust the speed of a clip.
- **Speed/Duration Settings**: Access the speed/duration options to set the precise playback speed percentage.
- **Time Remapping**: Advanced editing software allows for keyframe-based speed changes, known as time remapping.

C. Steps to Adjust Speed:

1. **Select the Clip**: Choose the clip in your timeline that you want to adjust.
2. **Rate Stretch Tool**: Activate the rate stretch tool (shortcut "R" in Premiere Pro) and drag the edge of the clip to adjust its speed.
3. **Speed/Duration Settings**: Right-click on the clip and select "Speed/Duration." Enter the desired speed percentage (e.g., 200% for double speed, 50% for half speed).
4. **Time Remapping**: For more advanced control, use the time remapping feature to add keyframes and adjust the clip's speed over time.

D. Common Speed Adjustments:

- **Speed Up**: Increase the playback speed to create fast-motion effects. Useful for time-lapses, accelerating slow scenes, or creating playful effects.
- **Slow Down**: Decrease the playback speed to emphasize details and create dramatic moments. Ideal for action sequences, sports highlights, or emotional scenes.

2. Slow Motion

A. Understanding Slow Motion:

- **Definition**: Slow motion involves playing back footage at a slower rate than it was recorded. This effect highlights details and actions that might be missed at normal speed.
- **Purpose**: Slow motion adds drama, suspense, and emphasis to specific moments. It's commonly used in sports, cinematic scenes, and artistic videos.

B. Recording for Slow Motion:

- **High Frame Rate Recording**: To achieve smooth slow motion, record your footage at a higher frame rate than your intended playback rate. For example, record at 120 fps for playback at 30 fps.
- **Resolution and Shutter Speed**: Ensure you maintain the resolution and adjust the shutter speed to match the frame rate (e.g., 1/240 for 120 fps).

C. Creating Slow Motion in Editing:

1. **Import High Frame Rate Footage**: Ensure you have high frame rate footage imported into your project.
2. **Set Playback Speed**: Adjust the playback speed of your high frame rate footage to achieve the slow-motion effect. For example, set a 120 fps clip to play at 30 fps for 1/4 speed.
3. **Time Remapping**: Fine-tune the slow-motion effect using time remapping to vary the speed gradually.

D. Ensuring Smooth Slow Motion:

- **Optical Flow/Frame Blending**: Use optical flow or frame blending options in your editing software to interpolate frames and create smooth slow motion.
- **Motion Blur**: Apply motion blur effects to enhance the realism and fluidity of the slow-motion footage.

3. Best Practices for Speed Adjustments and Slow Motion

A. Plan Your Shots: When recording footage, consider which scenes you might want to adjust the speed of or apply slow motion to. Record at higher frame rates for these scenes. **B. Test Different Speeds**: Experiment with different speed adjustments to achieve the desired effect. Preview your changes to ensure they fit the overall mood and flow of your project. **C. Maintain Quality**: Use high-quality footage and ensure your editing software's optical flow or frame blending settings are optimized for the best results. **D. Combine Effects**: Enhance your speed adjustments with other effects, such as color grading or sound design, to create a cohesive and impactful final product. **E. Use Judiciously**: Speed adjustments and slow motion can be powerful tools, but use them sparingly to avoid overdoing the effect and overwhelming your audience.

By mastering speed adjustments and slow-motion techniques, you can add depth and creativity to your video projects, making them more engaging and visually appealing.

Green Screen and Chroma Key Techniques

Using green screen (also known as chroma keying) is a powerful technique that allows you to replace the background of your footage with a different image or video. Here's a detailed guide on how to effectively use green screen and chroma key techniques:

1. Understanding Green Screen and Chroma Key

A. What is Green Screen?

- **Definition**: Green screen is a technique where a solid green background is used during filming, which can later be replaced with any image or video using chroma keying.
- **Purpose**: It allows for seamless integration of different backgrounds, special effects, and virtual environments in post-production.

B. Why Green?

- **Contrast**: Green is chosen because it contrasts well with most human skin tones and clothing. It also requires less lighting compared to blue screens.
- **Color Spillage**: Green produces less color spill on subjects, making it easier to key out.

2. Preparing for Green Screen Filming

A. Setting Up the Green Screen:

1. **Smooth Surface**: Ensure the green screen is smooth, without wrinkles or creases, to avoid shadows and uneven lighting.
2. **Proper Lighting**: Evenly light the green screen to avoid hotspots and shadows. Use soft, diffused lighting to achieve an even backdrop.

B. Lighting the Subject:

1. **Separate Lighting**: Light the subject separately from the green screen to avoid shadows and color spill.
2. **Use Backlights**: Use backlights or rim lights to create a clear separation between the subject and the green screen.

C. Camera Settings:

1. **Camera Position**: Maintain a reasonable distance between the subject and the green screen to prevent shadows and ensure even keying.
2. **Shutter Speed and Aperture**: Maintain proper exposure settings to avoid overexposure or underexposure, which can affect the keying process.

3. Keying Out the Green Screen in Editing

A. Importing Footage:

1. **Load the Clips**: Import your green screen footage and the background footage into your editing software.

B. Applying the Chroma Key Effect:

1. **Add Chroma Key Effect**: Apply the chroma key effect to

the green screen footage. In Adobe Premiere Pro, this is called Ultra Key, while in Final Cut Pro, it's simply called Keyer.

2. **Select Key Color**: Use the eyedropper tool to select the green color on the screen. This will remove the green background.

C. Fine-Tuning the Key:

1. **Adjust Parameters**: Fine-tune the keying effect by adjusting parameters such as threshold, tolerance, and edge blend to achieve a clean and natural look.

2. **Suppress Spill**: Use spill suppression controls to remove any remaining green color around the edges of the subject.

D. Adding the Background:

1. **Place Background Layer**: Add the desired background image or video onto the timeline, placing it directly below the green screen footage.

2. **Scale and Position**: Adjust the scale and position of the background as needed to create a seamless composite.

4. Advanced Chroma Key Techniques

A. Keying Out Complex Backgrounds:

1. **Use Masks**: Apply masks to isolate the areas where keying is challenging. This helps refine the key and improve the overall result.

2. **Multiple Pass Keying**: Perform multiple keying passes for complex shots with varying shades of green.

B. Creating Realistic Composites:

1. **Match Lighting and Color**: Adjust the lighting and color of the background to match the subject, creating a cohesive and realistic composite.

2. **Add Shadows and Reflections**: Integrate realistic shadows and reflections to enhance the believability of the composite.

C. Working with Motion Tracking:

1. **Track Movement**: Use motion tracking to ensure the background moves naturally with the subject, especially in dynamic scenes.

2. **Apply Keyframes**: Animate the position, scale, and rotation of the background to match the subject's movement for a seamless effect.

5. Common Challenges and Solutions

A. Uneven Lighting and Hotspots: Use soft, diffused lighting and adjust the position of lights to eliminate hotspots and achieve even illumination. **B. Green Spill**: Adjust spill suppression settings and use backlighting to reduce green spill on the subject. **C. Poor Keying Results**: Fine-tune keying parameters, use masks, and apply multiple passes if needed to improve keying quality.

By mastering green screen and chroma key techniques, you can unlock endless creative possibilities, seamlessly integrating subjects into virtually any environment.

CHAPTER 6: AUDIO EDITING AND MIXING

Importing and Syncing Audio

Effective audio editing and mixing are crucial for creating professional-quality videos. Here's a detailed guide to help you import and sync audio efficiently:

1. Importing Audio

A. Types of Audio Files:

- **Dialogue**: Recorded conversations, interviews, and voiceovers.
- **Music**: Background music, soundtracks, and musical effects.
- **Sound Effects**: Foley sounds, ambient noises, and special effects.

B. Preparing Audio Files:

1. **Organize Files**: Before importing, organize your audio files into clearly labeled folders (e.g., Dialogue, Music, SFX).
2. **Backup Files**: Ensure all audio files are backed up to prevent data loss.

C. Importing into Editing Software:

1. **Open Your Project**: Launch your editing software and open your project or create a new one.
2. **Import Audio Files**:
    - **Manual Import**: Go to the 'File' menu, select

'Import' or 'Import Media,' and navigate to your audio files.

- **Drag and Drop**: Drag your audio files directly from the file explorer into the project's media bin or library within the software.

3. **Organize Imported Files**: Place imported audio files into respective bins or folders within your project (e.g., create separate bins for Dialogue, Music, and SFX).

2. Syncing Audio

A. Manual Syncing:

1. **Aligning Clips**: Place the video and audio clips on separate tracks in the timeline.

2. **Visual Cues**: Use visual cues such as clapperboard marks or hand claps to align the audio waveform with the corresponding video frames.

3. **Fine-Tuning**: Zoom in on the timeline and fine-tune the alignment by adjusting the audio clip's position frame by frame until it matches perfectly.

B. Automatic Syncing:

1. **Sync by Timecode**: If your footage and audio have timecode metadata, use the sync-by-timecode feature available in professional editing software.

2. **Sync by Audio Waveform**: Many editing software offer automatic audio syncing that aligns video and audio clips based on their waveforms. Here's how to use it in popular editing tools:

   - **Adobe Premiere Pro**: Select the video and audio clips, right-click and choose 'Synchronize.' Choose the 'Audio' option and click 'OK.'

   - **Final Cut Pro**: Select the clips, right-click and choose 'Synchronize Clips' or use the 'Automatic Sync' feature.

   - **DaVinci Resolve**: Select the clips, right-click

and choose 'Auto Sync Audio' based on waveform.

C. Verifying Sync:

1. **Play and Review**: Play back the synced footage to ensure the audio and video are perfectly aligned.

2. **Adjust if Needed**: If any discrepancies are noticed, manually adjust the audio clip's position to achieve perfect synchronization.

3. Organizing and Editing Synced Audio

A. Using Tracks for Different Audio Elements:

1. **Dialogue Track**: Keep all dialogue clips on a dedicated audio track. This simplifies editing and ensures clarity.

2. **Music Track**: Place background music and soundtracks on a separate track for easy control over volume and transitions.

3. **SFX Track**: Assign sound effects to their own track, allowing precise placement and adjustments.

B. Applying Labels and Tags:

1. **Label Clips**: Use labels or color codes to distinguish between different types of audio files.

2. **Add Metadata**: Add metadata like descriptions, keywords, and markers to your audio clips for easier navigation and searching.

C. Editing and Adjusting Audio:

1. **Cutting and Trimming**: Use the razor tool to cut and trim audio clips to remove unwanted sections or adjust timing.

2. **Adjusting Levels**: Normalize audio levels to ensure consistency across all clips. Adjust volume levels using keyframes for dynamic changes.

3. **Adding Effects**: Apply audio effects such as equalization (EQ), reverb, and noise reduction to improve the overall

sound quality.

4. Best Practices

A. Monitor Audio Quality: Always use high-quality headphones or studio monitors to ensure accurate audio monitoring. **B. Maintain Consistency**: Ensure consistent audio levels across different clips to provide a smooth listening experience for your audience. **C. Backup Regularly**: Regularly save and back up your project files to prevent data loss.

By mastering the importing and syncing of audio, you can create seamless and professional videos that captivate your audience with both visual and auditory elements.

Basic Audio Adjustments and Filters

Effective audio adjustments and the use of filters are crucial for enhancing the quality and clarity of your video's sound. Here's a detailed guide to help you master these techniques:

1. Basic Audio Adjustments

A. Adjusting Volume Levels:

1. **Normalize Audio**: Ensure all audio clips have consistent volume levels by normalizing them. Most editing software has a normalize function that adjusts the audio clip to a target level.
2. **Gain Control**: Adjust the gain to increase or decrease the level of the audio clip without affecting its original quality. Use the gain setting in your software's audio mixer.

B. Keyframing Volume Changes:

1. **Set Keyframes**: Use keyframes to create dynamic volume changes within a clip. For example, gradually increase or decrease volume relative to the scene.
2. **Adjust Keyframes**: Place keyframes on the audio track where you want the volume change to begin and end. Adjust the keyframe levels as needed.

C. Balancing Audio Tracks:

1. **Dialogue vs. Background Music**: Balance dialogue and background music to ensure the dialogue is clear and audible. Lower the volume of the background music when dialogue is present.

2. **Sound Effects**: Adjust the levels of sound effects to ensure they complement and do not overpower the main audio.

D. Panning Audio:

1. **Stereo Experience**: Create a more dynamic stereo experience by panning audio elements. For example, pan a sound effect slightly to the left or right to match the on-screen action.

2. **Using Automation**: Use automation to pan audio seamlessly over time. This is useful for creating a sense of movement within the audio space.

2. Applying Audio Filters

A. Equalization (EQ):

1. **What is EQ?**: Equalization adjusts the balance between different frequency components within an audio signal.

2. **Applying EQ**: Use EQ filters to enhance or reduce specific frequencies. For example, boost the midrange to make dialogue clearer, or reduce low frequencies to remove rumble.

3. **Graphic vs. Parametric EQ**: Graphic EQ provides fixed frequency bands, while parametric EQ allows for precise control over frequency, bandwidth, and gain.

B. Compression:

1. **What is Compression?**: Compression reduces the dynamic range of audio, making quieter sounds louder and louder sounds quieter.

2. **Using Compression**: Apply compression to dialogue to maintain consistent volume levels. Adjust the

threshold and ratio settings to control the intensity of compression.

C. Noise Reduction:

1. **Removing Background Noise**: Use noise reduction filters to eliminate unwanted background noise. Most software provides tools to sample and reduce noise levels.

2. **Adaptive Noise Reduction**: Some tools offer adaptive noise reduction that dynamically adjusts to changing noise conditions.

D. Reverb and Delay:

1. **Creating Ambiance**: Use reverb and delay to add depth and space to your audio. These effects simulate the acoustic environment (e.g., room, hall, or cathedral).

2. **Adjusting Parameters**: Control parameters like decay time, pre-delay, and mix level to achieve the desired effect.

E. High-Pass and Low-Pass Filters:

1. **High-Pass Filter**: Allows frequencies above a certain threshold to pass through, removing lower frequencies. Useful for eliminating hum and rumble.

2. **Low-Pass Filter**: Allows frequencies below a certain threshold to pass through, removing higher frequencies. Often used to reduce sibilance or harshness.

3. Best Practices

A. Monitor Continuously: Always monitor your audio on high-quality headphones or studio monitors to ensure accurate adjustments. **B. Subtle Adjustments**: Start with subtle adjustments and gradually increase intensity. Overusing filters can distort the original audio quality. **C. Match the Scene**: Adjust audio based on the context and mood of the scene. Ensure all elements work harmoniously to create an immersive experience. **D. Test on Different Devices**: Test your audio mix on various devices (e.g., speakers, headphones, mobile) to ensure it sounds good across different playback systems.

By mastering basic audio adjustments and filters, you'll enhance the overall quality and professionalism of your video projects.

Adding Background Music and Sound Effects

Adding background music and sound effects can significantly enhance the emotional impact and overall quality of your videos. Here's a comprehensive guide on how to seamlessly integrate these elements into your projects:

1. Choosing the Right Background Music

A. Finding Suitable Music:

1. **Royalty-Free Music**: Use royalty-free music libraries like Epidemic Sound, Artlist, or AudioJungle to avoid copyright issues.

2. **Genre and Mood**: Select music that matches the tone and mood of your video. For example, use upbeat music for a lively scene or calm music for a reflective moment.

B. Preparing the Music:

1. **Trim and Edit**: Trim the music to fit the length of your video. Use fade-in and fade-out effects to smooth transitions.

2. **Matching the Beat**: Sync the music to the beats of your video, especially for action sequences or montages. Aligning cuts with musical beats can create a more dynamic and cohesive experience.

C. Adding Music to the Timeline:

1. **Import Music**: Import your chosen music track into your editing software's media bin.

2. **Place on Music Track**: Drag the music file onto a dedicated audio track in your timeline.

3. **Adjust Volume**: Ensure the background music doesn't overpower dialogue or sound effects. Use keyframes to

adjust the volume dynamically (e.g., lower the volume during dialogue).

2. Integrating Sound Effects

A. Types of Sound Effects:

1. **Foley**: Sounds created during post-production to mimic real-world noises (e.g., footsteps, door creaks).
2. **Ambient Sounds**: Background noises that set the scene (e.g., city sounds, nature).
3. **Impact Sounds**: Used to emphasize actions (e.g., punches, explosions).
4. **Creative Effects**: Unique or synthetic sounds used for stylistic purposes (e.g., whooshes, zips).

B. Finding Sound Effects:

1. **Sound Effect Libraries**: Access libraries like SoundSnap, freesound.org, or Splice for a wide range of sound effects.
2. **Recording Your Own**: Record custom sounds using a microphone for unique or specific effects.

C. Adding Sound Effects to the Timeline:

1. **Import Sound Effects**: Import the sound effect files into your editing software's media bin.
2. **Place on SFX Track**: Drag the sound effects onto a dedicated audio track in your timeline. Organize them based on type (e.g., Foley, ambient).
3. **Sync with Visuals**: Align sound effects precisely with the corresponding actions on screen. Zoom in on the timeline for finer control.
4. **Layering Effects**: Combine multiple sound effects to create a richer audio experience (e.g., layering ambient sounds with specific Foley effects).

3. Balancing Audio Elements

A. Volume Mixing:

1. **Dialogue Priority**: Ensure dialogue remains clear and intelligible by keeping its volume levels higher than background music and sound effects.

2. **Adjust Background Music**: Lower the volume of background music during dialogue sections and raise it during transitions or B-roll sequences.

3. **Balancing Sound Effects**: Adjust the volume of sound effects to ensure they are noticeable but not overpowering.

B. Using Audio Filters and Effects:

1. **Equalization (EQ)**: Use EQ to enhance or reduce specific frequencies in your music and sound effects for better clarity.

2. **Reverb and Delay**: Apply reverb and delay effects to create a sense of space and depth for ambient sounds.

3. **Compression and Limiting**: Use compression to balance dynamic ranges and limiting to prevent audio peaks from clipping.

C. Fine-Tuning with Keyframes:

1. **Volume Keyframes**: Use keyframes to automate volume changes, ensuring smooth transitions and balanced levels throughout your video.

2. **Pan Keyframes**: Pan audio elements left or right to match on-screen actions or to create a spatial audio experience.

4. Best Practices

A. Consistency: Maintain a consistent audio style throughout your project to provide a cohesive listening experience. **B. Subtlety**: Use sound effects subtly to enhance the narrative without distracting the viewer. **C. Test and Review**: Regularly test your audio mix on various playback devices to ensure it sounds good across different platforms.

By effectively adding background music and sound effects, you can elevate your video projects, making them more engaging and immersive.

Audio Transitions and Keyframes

Mastering audio transitions and keyframes is essential for creating a polished and professional audio mix in your videos. Here's a detailed guide on how to effectively use these techniques:

1. Audio Transitions

A. Understanding Audio Transitions:

- **Definition**: Audio transitions are used to smoothly connect one audio clip to another or to gradually introduce or remove sound elements.
- **Purpose**: They help create seamless audio experiences, enhance storytelling, and prevent abrupt changes in sound.

B. Common Types of Audio Transitions:

- **Crossfade**: Gradually lowers the volume of one clip while increasing the volume of the next. Useful for smooth transitions between music tracks or sound effects.
- **Fade In/Fade Out**: Gradually increases the volume at the start (fade in) or decreases the volume at the end (fade out) of a clip. Ideal for introducing or ending audio elements.
- **Constant Gain**: Fades audio at a constant rate, maintaining the perceived volume level. Useful for dialogue transitions.
- **Exponential Fade**: Creates a more natural fade by gradually changing the volume at an exponential rate.

C. Applying Audio Transitions:

1. **Select Transition**: Choose the desired transition from the audio effects or transition panel in your editing software.
2. **Drag and Drop**: Drag the transition onto the timeline,

placing it between two audio clips or at the start/end of a clip.

3. **Adjust Duration**: Lengthen or shorten the transition by dragging its edges on the timeline to achieve the desired effect.

4. **Fine-Tune Settings**: Use the transition settings panel to adjust parameters such as fade type, duration, and curve for more precise control.

2. Keyframes

A. Understanding Keyframes:

- **Definition**: Keyframes are markers that define the start and end points of any transition, controlling properties such as volume, pan, and effects over time.
- **Purpose**: They allow you to create dynamic audio changes, such as volume fades, pan movements, and effect adjustments throughout your timeline.

B. Basic Keyframing Techniques:

1. **Enable Keyframing**: Click the stopwatch icon next to the property you want to animate (e.g., volume) in the effects control panel.

2. **Adding Keyframes**: Move the playhead to the starting point of the audio change and set the first keyframe by adjusting the property value. Move the playhead to the end point and set the second keyframe by adjusting the property value to the desired state.

3. **Intermediate Keyframes**: Add additional keyframes between the start and end points for more complex audio adjustments.

C. Keyframing Volume Changes:

1. **Set Keyframes**: Use keyframes to adjust the volume property over time. For example, gradually fade in music or sound effects.

2. **Adjust Keyframe Levels**: Click and drag keyframes on

the timeline or use the effects control panel to fine-tune volume levels and transitions.

D. Keyframing Pan Movements:

1. **Set Pan Keyframes**: Use keyframes to control the pan property, moving audio elements left or right within the stereo field.

2. **Create Dynamic Panning**: Animate the pan property over time to create a sense of movement or spatial audio effects.

E. Keyframing Effects:

1. **Enable Keyframing for Effects**: Apply effects like reverb, EQ, or delay, and use keyframes to adjust their parameters over time.

2. **Animate Effects**: Create subtle or dramatic changes in effects to enhance the audio experience and match on-screen actions.

3. Best Practices for Audio Transitions and Keyframes

A. Smooth Transitions: Use crossfades and fades to ensure smooth transitions between audio clips, avoiding abrupt changes.
B. Consistent Levels: Maintain consistent audio levels to ensure dialogue, music, and sound effects are balanced and clear.
C. Precise Control: Utilize keyframes for precise control over volume, pan, and effects, allowing for dynamic and expressive audio adjustments. **D. Test and Review**: Regularly review your audio mix to ensure transitions and keyframed changes sound natural and cohesive.

By mastering audio transitions and keyframes, you can enhance the overall quality and professionalism of your video projects, creating a seamless and immersive audio experience for your audience.

CHAPTER 7: COLOR CORRECTION AND GRADING

Introduction to Color Theory

An understanding of color theory is essential for successful color correction and grading in video editing. Here's an introduction to the fundamental concepts of color theory:

1. The Color Wheel

A. Primary Colors:

- **Red, Green, Blue (RGB)**: Primary colors of light used in digital screens and video editing. Combining these colors in various ways creates all other colors.

- **Cyan, Magenta, Yellow (CMY)**: Secondary colors formed by mixing two primary colors.

B. Secondary Colors:

- **Cyan**: Created by combining green and blue.

- **Magenta**: Created by combining red and blue.

- **Yellow**: Created by combining red and green.

C. Tertiary Colors:

- **Mixing Primary and Secondary Colors**: Tertiary colors are formed by mixing a primary color with a secondary color, resulting in hues like red-orange, yellow-green, and blue-violet.

D. Complementary Colors:

- **Opposite on the Color Wheel**: Complementary colors are opposite each other on the color wheel (e.g., red and green, blue and orange). They create high contrast and vibrant looks when used together.

2. Color Properties

A. Hue:

- **Definition**: The name of the color (e.g., red, blue, yellow). It is determined by the wavelength of light.
- **Application**: Adjusting the hue alters the actual color of your footage.

B. Saturation:

- **Definition**: The intensity or purity of a color. High saturation means vivid, bright colors; low saturation means muted, grey tones.
- **Application**: Adjusting saturation affects how vivid or dull a color appears.

C. Luminance (Brightness):

- **Definition**: The amount of light emitted or reflected by a color. High luminance means a light color; low luminance means a dark color.
- **Application**: Adjusting luminance changes the brightness or darkness of your footage.

3. Color Harmony

A. Analogous Colors:

- **Definition**: Colors that are next to each other on the color wheel (e.g., blue, blue-green, green). They create harmonious and pleasing combinations.
- **Application**: Useful for creating a cohesive and visually appealing look.

B. Triadic Colors:

- **Definition**: Three colors that are evenly spaced around the color wheel (e.g., red, yellow, blue). They create a balanced and vibrant look.

- **Application**: Often used to achieve bold and dynamic visuals.

C. Split-Complementary Colors:

- **Definition**: A base color and two adjacent colors to its complement (e.g., red, blue-green, yellow-green). They offer contrast while maintaining harmony.
- **Application**: Ideal for creating contrast without the intensity of direct complementary colors.

4. Color Temperature

A. Warm Colors:

- **Definition**: Colors on the red, orange, and yellow side of the color wheel. They often evoke warmth and energy.
- **Application**: Use warm colors to create inviting and energetic scenes.

B. Cool Colors:

- **Definition**: Colors on the blue, green, and violet side of the color wheel. They often evoke calmness and serenity.
- **Application**: Use cool colors to create calming and peaceful scenes.

C. White Balance:

- **Definition**: Adjusting the overall color balance to ensure whites appear white and colors are accurate.
- **Application**: Essential for maintaining color accuracy in your footage.

5. Practical Applications

A. Color Correction:

1. **Purpose**: Corrects any color inaccuracies caused by lighting conditions, camera settings, or other factors.
2. **Techniques**: Adjust white balance, correct saturation, and luminance levels, and match colors across different shots.

B. Color Grading:

1. **Purpose**: Enhances the visual style and mood of your video, creating a specific atmosphere or artistic look.
2. **Techniques**: Use color wheels, LUTs (Look-Up Tables), and grading panels in your editing software to achieve the desired effect.

C. Tools and Software:

1. **Adobe Premiere Pro**: Equipped with Lumetri Color panels for comprehensive color correction and grading.
2. **DaVinci Resolve**: Industry-standard software known for its exceptional color grading capabilities.
3. **Final Cut Pro**: Offers robust color grading tools and seamless workflow integration.

By understanding color theory, you can make informed decisions during color correction and grading, ensuring your video projects look polished and professional.

Basic Color Correction Techniques

Effective color correction ensures that the colors in your video appear natural and consistent, enhancing the overall quality and visual appeal. Here are some essential color correction techniques to get you started:

1. Understanding Color Correction

A. Difference Between Color Correction and Color Grading:

- **Color Correction**: Involves adjusting colors to achieve a natural and realistic look, correcting issues caused by lighting or camera settings.
- **Color Grading**: Enhances or alters the visual style and mood of a video, adding an artistic touch.

2. Using Color Correction Tools

A. Scopes and Monitors:

- **Waveform Monitor**: Displays luminance (brightness)

levels. Use it to ensure proper exposure and balance of highlights and shadows.

- **Vectorscope**: Shows color information. Use it to analyze color balance and saturation.
- **Histogram**: Displays the distribution of light across shadows, midtones, and highlights.

B. Basic Color Correction Workflow:

STEP 1: ADJUST EXPOSURE

1. **Correct Luminance Levels**: Use the waveform monitor to adjust the brightness of your footage, ensuring that highlights are not overexposed and shadows are not underexposed.

2. **Lift, Gamma, Gain**: Use these primary controls to adjust blacks (lift), midtones (gamma), and whites (gain) individually.

STEP 2: BALANCE COLOR

1. **White Balance**: Correct the color temperature to ensure whites appear neutral. Adjust the white balance slider to remove any color cast (e.g., blue or orange tint).
2. **Tent and Tint**: Use the tent and tint controls to fine-tune color balance, correcting any residual color shifts.

STEP 3: ADJUST SATURATION

1. **Enhance or Reduce Saturation**: Adjust the saturation level to make colors more vivid or muted, depending on the desired look.

2. **Avoid Over-Saturation**: Ensure that the colors remain natural and do not appear too intense unless it is a stylistic choice.

STEP 4: MATCH SHOTS

1. **Consistency**: Ensure that color correction is consistent across all shots in a sequence. Compare adjacent shots to maintain a seamless flow.

2. **Shot Matching Tools**: Use automatic shot matching tools available in your editing software to help achieve consistency.

3. Detailed Color Correction Techniques

A. Primary Color Correction:

Exposure Adjustment:

1. **Black Level (Lift)**: Adjust to ensure black areas are truly black without losing shadow detail.

2. **Midtones (Gamma)**: Adjust to ensure skin tones and midrange colors appear natural.

3. **Highlight Level (Gain)**: Adjust to ensure white areas are truly white without losing highlight detail.

White Balance Adjustment:

1. **Setting the Neutral**: Use the white balance picker to select a neutral color (e.g., grey or white) in the frame.

2. **Manual Adjustment**: Fine-tune the white balance manually using temperature and tint sliders.

B. Secondary Color Correction:

Selective Adjustments:

1. **Color Wheels**: Use color wheels to make fine adjustments to shadows, midtones, and highlights individually.

2. **Hue vs. Hue, Hue vs. Sat, Hue vs. Luma**: Use these advanced curves to make precise adjustments to specific colors or ranges in the image.

Example Workflow in Adobe Premiere Pro:

1. **Lumetri Color Panel**: Use the Lumetri Color Panel to access primary and secondary color correction tools.

2. **Basic Correction**: Adjust white balance, exposure, contrast, highlights, shadows, whites, and blacks under the Basic Correction tab.

3. **Curves**: Use the Curves tab for more detailed adjustments to specific color ranges.

4. **Color Wheels & Match**: Adjust shadows, midtones, and highlights under the Color Wheels & Match tab for secondary corrections.

4. Best Practices for Color Correction

A. Use Reference Monitors: Reference monitors provide accurate color representation, helping you make precise adjustments. **B. Work in a Controlled Environment**: Edit in a room with consistent lighting and neutral-colored walls to avoid color casting. **C. Regularly Calibrate Your Monitor**: Ensure your monitor is calibrated regularly for accurate color representation. **D. Keep it Natural**: Aim for natural-looking colors that enhance the visual appeal without appearing artificial.

By mastering basic color correction techniques, you'll significantly improve the quality and professionalism of your video projects, ensuring they look polished and visually pleasing.

Advanced Color Grading Tools

Advanced color grading tools offer precision and flexibility, enabling you to create visually stunning videos that convey the desired mood and style. Here's a comprehensive guide to some of the most powerful color grading tools available:

1. Color Wheels and Match

A. Color Wheels:

- **Shadows, Midtones, and Highlights**: Adjust the hue and saturation levels for shadows, midtones, and highlights separately. This allows for targeted grading and improved color balance throughout the image.
- **Lift, Gamma, Gain**: Commonly found in color wheels, these controls let you adjust the blacks (lift), midtones (gamma), and whites (gain).

B. Color Match:

- **Automatic Matching**: Many editing software tools offer automatic color matching features that help achieve consistent color grading across different shots. This is particularly useful for maintaining continuity in scenes shot under varying lighting conditions.

2. Curves

A. RGB Curves:

- **Overview**: Adjust the brightness and contrast of specific color channels (Red, Green, Blue) or the overall luminance (Master) using curves.
- **Applications**: Use to correct color imbalances, enhance contrast, and create custom looks by manipulating the tonal range.

B. HSL Curves:

- **Hue vs. Hue**: Adjust a specific hue in your image to another hue.
- **Hue vs. Saturation**: Increase or decrease the saturation of specific hues.
- **Hue vs. Luma**: Adjust the luminance of specific colors, useful for balancing the brightness of different hues.

3. LUTs (Look-Up Tables)

A. Understanding LUTs:

- **Definition**: LUTs are pre-configured color settings that can be applied to your footage to achieve a specific look or style.

. **Purpose**: Simplify the color grading process by providing a starting point for further adjustments.

B. Application:

1. **Choose LUT**: Select an appropriate LUT from the library or import custom LUTs.

2. **Apply LUT**: Apply the LUT to your footage in the color grading panel.

3. **Fine-Tune**: Adjust the intensity and refine the look using additional color grading tools to tailor it to your needs.

4. Secondary Color Correction

A. Isolating Colors:

. **Qualifiers**: Use qualifiers to isolate specific colors or regions, allowing for precise adjustments. This is useful for making detailed changes to specific parts of the image.

. **Masks and Power Windows**: Apply masks to limit color corrections to specific areas within the frame. Power windows are often used in software like DaVinci Resolve to create custom shapes for targeted grading.

B. Adjustments within Selected Areas:

. **HSL Qualifiers**: Use HSL (Hue, Saturation, Luminance) qualifiers to target specific color ranges in your image.

. **Rotten Correction**: Correct or enhance specific colors without affecting the entire frame.

5. Keyframes and Animation

A. Dynamic Color Changes:

. **Keyframing**: Animate color grading adjustments over time using keyframes. This allows for gradual changes in color and lighting to match the progression of your scene.

- **Scene Transitions**: Use keyframes to create smooth transitions between different color grades in consecutive scenes.

B. Applying Keyframes:

1. **Set Initial Keyframe**: Move the playhead to the start of the desired color change and set the first keyframe.

2. **Adjust Parameters**: Move the playhead to the end of the change and set another keyframe with the adjusted color parameters.

3. **Preview and Refine**: Play back the animation and make any necessary adjustments to ensure a smooth transition.

6. Advanced Tools and Plugins

A. HDR Grading:

- **High Dynamic Range (HDR)**: Use HDR grading tools to enhance the dynamic range, allowing for greater detail in highlights and shadows.

- **HDR Scopes**: Utilize HDR-specific scopes to monitor and adjust the expanded luminance range accurately.

B. Noise Reduction and Sharpening:

- **Noise Reduction**: Apply noise reduction tools to clean up footage and reduce graininess, especially in low-light scenes.

- **Sharpening**: Use sharpening filters to enhance the clarity and detail of your footage. Adjust settings carefully to avoid introducing artifacts.

C. Popular Plugins:

- **Magic Bullet Looks**: A powerful plugin for creating cinematic looks with a wide range of presets and customization options.

- **FilmConvert**: Simulates the appearance of different film stocks, adding a unique and professional touch to your video projects.

By mastering advanced color grading tools, you can achieve a professional and cinematic look for your videos, enhancing their visual storytelling and emotional impact.

Creating and Applying LUTs

Look-Up Tables (LUTs) are powerful tools that can help you achieve consistent and stylized colors in your videos. Here's a detailed guide on how to create and apply LUTs:

1. Understanding LUTs

A. What is a LUT?

- **Definition**: A LUT (Look-Up Table) is a pre-configured mapping that adjusts the colors of an image. It translates input color values to desired output color values, allowing for consistent color grading.
- **Purpose**: LUTs are used to apply specific looks or styles, make color corrections, or quickly achieve a consistent color grade across multiple clips.

B. Types of LUTs:

- **Technical LUTs**: Used for color correction and calibration, ensuring accurate color reproduction.
- **Creative LUTs**: Applied to achieve stylized looks or enhance the mood of a video. Examples include film emulation LUTs and thematic color grades.

2. Creating LUTs

A. Using Color Grading Software:

1. **Select a Grading Tool**: Use professional color grading software like Adobe Premiere Pro, DaVinci Resolve, or Final Cut Pro.
2. **Grade Your Footage**: Apply color corrections and adjustments to achieve the desired look. Use tools like color wheels, curves, and HSL adjustments.

3. **Save the Look**: Once satisfied with the grade, save the color adjustments as a LUT. This process typically involves exporting the current color grade as a .cube file or another standard LUT format.

B. Customize and Refine:

1. **Test the LUT**: Apply the LUT to different clips to ensure it consistently delivers the desired look. Make adjustments as needed.

2. **Iterate**: Refine the LUT based on feedback and testing, ensuring it works well across various lighting conditions and scenes.

3. Applying LUTs

A. Importing LUTs into Editing Software:

1. **Adobe Premiere Pro**:
   - **Open Lumetri Color Panel**: Go to the Color workspace and open the Lumetri Color panel.
   - **Input LUT**: Under the Basic Correction tab, click on the Input LUT dropdown and select "Browse." Navigate to your LUT file and apply it.
   - **Creative LUT**: Under the Creative tab, use the Look dropdown to apply a creative LUT. Fine-tune the intensity using the sliders.

2. **DaVinci Resolve**:
   - **Open Color Page**: Go to the Color page and open the LUT panel.
   - **Import LUT**: Right-click in the LUT panel and select "Import LUT." Navigate to your LUT file and import it.
   - **Apply LUT**: Drag and drop the LUT onto a node in the node tree or apply it directly to your clips.

3. **Final Cut Pro**:
   - **Open Effects Browser**: Go to the Effects browser

and search for the "Custom LUT" effect.

- ◦ **Apply LUT Effect**: Drag the Custom LUT effect onto the clip in the timeline.
- ◦ **Choose LUT**: In the Video Inspector, click on the LUT dropdown and select "Choose Custom LUT." Navigate to your LUT file and apply it.

B. Adjusting LUTs:

1. **Fine-Tune Intensity**: Adjust the intensity or opacity of the LUT to achieve the desired look. This ensures the LUT enhances your footage without overpowering it.
2. **Combine with Additional Adjustments**: Apply further color corrections and adjustments after applying the LUT to fine-tune the look. Use tools like color wheels, curves, and HSL adjustments to make precise changes.

C. Managing LUTs:

1. **Organize LUT Library**: Keep your LUTs organized in clearly labeled folders for easy access. Categorize them by purpose (e.g., technical, creative, film emulation) or project.
2. **Backup and Share**: Save backups of your LUTs on external drives or cloud storage. Share your LUTs with collaborators to maintain consistency across projects.

4. Best Practices for Using LUTs

A. Test Before Applying: Always test your LUTs on sample footage before applying them to an entire project. Ensure they deliver the desired look across different scenes. **B. Subtle Adjustments**: Use LUTs as a starting point and make subtle adjustments to refine the look. Avoid relying solely on LUTs for the final grade. **C. Consistency**: Apply LUTs consistently across your clips to maintain a cohesive visual style throughout your video. **D. Review on Different Monitors**: Check your color grade on various monitors to ensure it looks good across different display devices.

By mastering the creation and application of LUTs, you can

efficiently achieve consistent and professional-looking color grades in your video projects, enhancing their visual storytelling and emotional impact.

CHAPTER 8: ADDING TEXT AND GRAPHICS

Creating Titles and Lower Thirds

Titles and lower thirds are essential elements in video editing, used to provide context, introduce speakers, or add stylistic touches to your content. Here's a comprehensive guide on how to create effective titles and lower thirds:

1. Introduction to Titles and Lower Thirds

A. Titles:

- **Definition**: Titles are text overlays that appear at the beginning or within a video, often used for introductions, chapters, or key points.
- **Purpose**: They help convey important information, provide context, and enhance the visual appeal of your video.

B. Lower Thirds:

- **Definition**: Lower thirds are text graphics placed in the lower third of the screen, typically used to introduce speakers, locations, or additional information.
- **Purpose**: They add professionalism to your video by providing clear and concise information without distracting from the main content.

2. Creating Titles

A. Using Editing Software:

1. **Adobe Premiere Pro**:
   - **Text Tool**: Use the Type Tool to add text directly

to the timeline. Customize the font, size, color, and other properties in the Essential Graphics panel.

- ◦ **Templates**: Use built-in title templates from the Essential Graphics panel or import custom templates for a consistent look.

2. **Final Cut Pro**:

- ◦ **Text Tool**: Use the Text tool to add text to the timeline. Customize the text properties in the Text Inspector.
- ◦ **Motion Templates**: Utilize Motion templates for advanced title animation.

3. **DaVinci Resolve**:

- ◦ **Text Tool**: Add text using the Text tool in the Edit or Fusion tab. Customize properties in the Inspector.
- ◦ **Fusion Compositing**: Use the Fusion tab for advanced text animation and effects.

B. Customizing Titles:

1. **Font and Style**: Choose a font that matches the tone of your video. Use bold or italic styles for emphasis.

2. **Color and Opacity**: Select colors that complement your video's color scheme. Adjust opacity for subtle or bold text.

3. **Positioning**: Place titles in a prominent location on screen. Center-aligned titles work well for introductions, while corner-aligned titles can add stylistic flair.

4. **Animation**: Add animation effects like fade-in, fade-out, or slide-in to make titles more engaging.

3. Creating Lower Thirds

A. Using Editing Software:

1. **Adobe Premiere Pro**:

- **Essential Graphics Panel**: Use the Essential Graphics panel to create and customize lower thirds. Choose from built-in templates or create your own.
- **Keyframe Animation**: Animate the position and opacity of lower thirds using keyframes for smooth transitions.

2. **Final Cut Pro**:
   - **Text Tool**: Use the Text tool and built-in lower third templates in the Titles and Generators browser.
   - **Motion Graphics**: Utilize Motion for advanced customization and animation of lower thirds.

3. **DaVinci Resolve**:
   - **Text Tool**: Add text and use built-in lower third templates in the Edit or Fusion tab.
   - **Fusion Compositing**: Create custom lower thirds with advanced animation using the Fusion tab.

B. Customizing Lower Thirds:

1. **Text Information**: Include the speaker's name, title, and relevant details. Keep the text concise and easy to read.
2. **Design Elements**: Add background bars, lines, or shapes to enhance the visual appeal. Use colors and styles that match your video's theme.
3. **Branding**: Incorporate logos or branding elements to reinforce your company or channel's identity.
4. **Animation**: Use keyframes to animate lower thirds, such as sliding in from the side or fading in and out.

4. Best Practices for Titles and Lower Thirds

A. Consistency: Maintain consistent font styles, colors, and animation throughout your video. This ensures a cohesive and professional look. **B. Readability**: Choose fonts and colors that are easy to read on screen. Avoid overly decorative fonts that may distract from the content. **C. Placement**: Position titles and lower thirds where they won't obscure important visuals. Lower thirds should be placed at the bottom of the screen, leaving enough space for the main content. **D. Timing**: Ensure titles and lower thirds appear and disappear at appropriate times. They should remain on screen long enough to be read, but not linger unnecessarily.

By mastering the creation of titles and lower thirds, you can add professionalism and clarity to your video projects, enhancing their overall impact and viewer engagement.

Working with Motion Graphics and Animations

Motion graphics and animations add dynamic visual elements to your video projects, making them more engaging and visually appealing. Here's a comprehensive guide on how to create and work with motion graphics and animations:

1. Understanding Motion Graphics and Animations

A. Definition:

- **Motion Graphics**: Graphics that use motion to convey information. They often include text, shapes, and visual elements animated to create movement and visual interest.
- **Animations**: The process of creating movement through a series of still images or frames. In video editing, animations can be applied to text, graphics, and other visual elements.

B. Purpose:

- **Enhance Visual Appeal**: Motion graphics and animations make videos more engaging and visually interesting.
- **Convey Information**: They help in visualizing complex information, making it easier to understand.
- **Add Professionalism**: Well-designed animations and

motion graphics give videos a professional and polished look.

2. Creating Motion Graphics

A. Tools and Software:

1. **Adobe After Effects**: Industry-standard software for creating motion graphics and visual effects. It offers robust tools for animation, compositing, and special effects.
2. **Adobe Premiere Pro**: Includes Essential Graphics panel for creating simple motion graphics directly within the editing timeline.
3. **DaVinci Resolve**: Provides Fusion tab for advanced motion graphics and compositing.
4. **Final Cut Pro**: Integrates with Motion for creating detailed motion graphics and animations.

B. Basic Techniques:

1. **Animating Text:**
   - **Text Layers**: Create text layers and animate properties like position, scale, rotation, and opacity.
   - **Keyframes**: Set keyframes to define the start and end points of the animation. Adjust the timing and easing to achieve smooth motion.
   - **Presets**: Use text animation presets for quick and professional results.

2. **Animating Shapes and Graphics:**
   - **Shape Layers**: Create and animate shape layers, such as circles, rectangles, and custom paths.
   - **Transform Properties**: Animate position, scale, rotation, and opacity to create movement.
   - **Masks**: Use masks to animate the reveal or hide parts of a graphic.

3. **Using Expressions**: In software like After Effects, use expressions to automate animations and create complex motion with minimal keyframes.

3. Advanced Animation Techniques

A. Animation Principles:

1. **Easing**: Use easing to create natural acceleration and deceleration in animations. Apply ease-in, ease-out, or both for smooth transitions.

2. **Timing and Spacing**: Adjust timing and spacing of keyframes to create realistic motion. Experiment with different intervals to achieve the desired effect.

3. **Secondary Animation**: Add secondary animations to enhance realism. For example, animate a character's hair or clothing to follow the primary motion.

B. Using Graph Editors:

1. **Speed Graph**: Adjust the speed and timing of keyframes using the speed graph to create more dynamic animations.

2. **Value Graph**: Manipulate the value graph to control the specific properties of the animation, such as position or scale over time.

C. Working with 3D:

1. **3D Layers**: Enable 3D layers to animate objects in three-dimensional space.

2. **Cameras and Lights**: Use virtual cameras and lights to create realistic 3D scenes. Animate camera movements and light properties to enhance the visual depth.

4. Adding Motion Graphics to Your Project

A. Importing Motion Graphics:

1. **Dynamic Link**: Use Dynamic Link in Adobe apps to seamlessly import After Effects compositions into Premiere Pro without rendering.

2. **Export and Import**: Export motion graphics as video files or image sequences and import them into your editing project.

B. Integrating with Video:

1. **Blend Modes**: Use blend modes to seamlessly integrate motion graphics with your video footage.

2. **Layering**: Place motion graphics on separate layers above your video clips on the timeline. Adjust opacity and position for a harmonious blend.

3. **Color and Effects Matching**: Ensure motion graphics match the color grading and visual style of your video for consistency.

5. Best Practices for Motion Graphics and Animations

A. Keep it Simple: Avoid overloading your video with too many motion graphics and animations. Use them to enhance the story, not distract from it. **B. Consistency**: Maintain a consistent style and animation speed throughout your project to ensure a cohesive look. **C. Focus on Timing**: Pay attention to the timing of your animations to ensure they align with the flow and pace of your video. **D. Preview and Refine**: Regularly preview your animations and make adjustments as needed to achieve smooth and polished results. **E. Save Templates**: Save frequently used motion graphics as templates to streamline your workflow in future projects.

By mastering motion graphics and animation techniques, you can add depth, creativity, and professionalism to your video projects, capturing your audience's attention and enhancing the overall viewing experience.

Using Templates and Presets

Templates and presets are invaluable tools in video editing, allowing you to streamline your workflow and maintain consistency across your projects. Here's a detailed guide on how to effectively use templates and presets:

1. Understanding Templates and Presets

A. Templates:

- **Definition**: Pre-designed layouts or sequences that can be customized to fit your project needs. They often include placeholders for text, graphics, and media.
- **Purpose**: Save time and ensure consistency by providing a ready-made structure for common elements like titles, lower thirds, intros, and outros.

B. Presets:

- **Definition**: Pre-configured settings for effects, transitions, and animations that can be applied to your clips with a single click.
- **Purpose**: Streamline the application of frequently used effects and transitions, ensuring uniformity and saving time.

2. Using Templates

A. Applying Templates:

1. **Adobe Premiere Pro**:
   - **Essential Graphics Panel**: Navigate to the Essential Graphics panel to find and apply templates for titles, lower thirds, and other graphics.
   - **Customization**: Modify the text, colors, and other elements within the template to fit your project's style.
   - **Additional Templates**: Download additional templates from resources like Adobe Stock or create your own for future use.

2. **Final Cut Pro**:
   - **Titles and Generators Browser**: Access a variety of pre-built templates in the Titles and Generators browser.

- **Motion Templates**: Utilize Motion to create or customize templates and import them into Final Cut Pro for easy use.

3. **DaVinci Resolve:**
   - **Fusion Templates**: Use Fusion templates for advanced motion graphics and compositing. Customize templates within the Fusion tab.
   - **Edit Page**: Apply simpler templates directly in the Edit page for titles and lower thirds.

B. Customizing Templates:

1. **Text and Fonts**: Change the placeholder text to your desired content, selecting appropriate fonts and styles.
2. **Colors and Themes**: Adjust the colors and themes to match your project's branding or visual identity.
3. **Animation and Timing**: Edit the animation and timing of the template elements to align with your video's pacing.

C. Creating Custom Templates:

1. **Design Custom Templates**: Create your own templates that include frequently used graphics and animations. Save them for future projects to maintain consistency.
2. **Sharing Templates**: Share your custom templates with team members to ensure a unified style across collaborative projects.

3. Using Presets

A. Applying Presets:

1. **Adobe Premiere Pro:**
   - **Effect Controls**: Browse and apply presets from the Effect Controls panel. Customize parameters for specific effects like color correction, transitions, and keyframing.
   - **Save Custom Presets**: Save your frequently

used effect settings as custom presets for quick application in future projects.

2. **Final Cut Pro**:

   ◦ **Effects Browser**: Access the Effects browser to find and apply presets. Adjust preset parameters in the Video Inspector.

   ◦ **Save Preset**: Save custom effect settings as presets for consistent use across different clips.

3. **DaVinci Resolve**:

   ◦ **Effects Library**: Use the Effects Library to find and apply presets for various effects and transitions.

   ◦ **Power Grades**: Save color grading settings as Power Grades in the Gallery for easy application to multiple clips.

B. Customizing Presets:

1. **Adjust Parameters**: Modify the preset parameters to suit your specific needs. This includes tweaking intensity, duration, and other effect settings.

2. **Combine Presets**: Apply multiple presets to a clip for layered effects. Adjust the order and blend to achieve the desired result.

3. **Fine-Tune**: After applying presets, fine-tune the settings to ensure they integrate seamlessly with your project.

4. Best Practices for Using Templates and Presets

A. Consistency: Use templates and presets consistently across your project to maintain a cohesive look and feel. This is especially important for branded content. **B. Efficiency**: Take advantage of the time-saving benefits of templates and presets by incorporating them into your regular workflow. **C. Customization**: Customizable templates and presets should be tailored to fit the specific needs of each project. Avoid using default settings without adjustments. **D. Organization**: Keep your templates and presets organized in clearly labeled folders. This makes them easy to find and apply when needed. **E. Backup and Share**: Save backups of your custom templates and presets. Share them with team members to ensure everyone can access and use them.

By effectively using templates and presets, you can streamline your video editing process, ensure consistency, and save valuable time.

Animating Text

Animating text can add visual interest and enhance the storytelling in your videos. Here's a detailed guide on how to animate text effectively:

1. Basic Text Animations

A. Tools and Software:

1. **Adobe After Effects**: Industry-standard software for creating detailed text animations.
2. **Adobe Premiere Pro**: Includes Essential Graphics panel for basic text animations.
3. **Final Cut Pro**: Provides tools for text animation within the Titles and Generators browser.
4. **DaVinci Resolve**: Offers Fusion tab for advanced text animations.

B. Applying Animations:

1. **Adobe After Effects**:
   - **Text Layers**: Create a new text layer and type your desired text.
   - **Transform Properties**: Animate properties like position, scale, rotation, and opacity using keyframes.
   - **Text Animator**: Use the Text Animator feature to apply complex animations to individual characters or words.

- **Presets**: Apply text animation presets for quick and professional results.

2. **Adobe Premiere Pro**:
   - **Essential Graphics Panel**: Use the Type tool to add text and customize it in the Essential Graphics panel.
   - **Keyframes**: Animate text properties in the Video Effects panel using keyframes.
   - **Templates**: Use motion graphics templates for premade text animations.

3. **Final Cut Pro**:
   - **Titles and Generators Browser**: Add text from the Titles and Generators browser and customize it in the Text Inspector.
   - **Keyframes**: Animate text properties with keyframes to create smooth transitions.

4. **DaVinci Resolve**:
   - **Edit and Fusion Tabs**: Add text and customize animations using the Edit or Fusion tabs.
   - **Text+ Tool**: Use the Text+ tool in Fusion for advanced text animations.

2. Advanced Text Animations

A. Creating Custom Animations:

1. **Animating Position**: Move text across the screen by animating the position property. Create smooth motion using keyframes and easing.

2. **Animating Scale**: Animate the scale property to make text grow or shrink. Use keyframes to define the start and end points.

3. **Animating Opacity**: Create fade-in and fade-out effects by animating the opacity property.

4. **Animating Rotation**: Rotate text to add dynamic

movement. Use keyframes to control the angle and timing of the rotation.

B. Using Animation Presets:

1. **Text Animation Presets**: Apply built-in animation presets for quick effects like typewriter, bounce, and more.

2. **Fine-Tuning Presets**: Customize the parameters of animation presets to better fit your project.

C. Adding Effects to Text Animations:

1. **Glow and Shadow**: Add glow or shadow effects to highlight text and make it stand out.

2. **Stroke and Fill**: Animate the stroke and fill properties of text to create unique visual effects.

3. **Motion Blur**: Apply motion blur to text animations for a more natural look.

3. Best Practices for Animating Text

A. Keep It Legible: Ensure that the text remains easy to read throughout the animation. Avoid overly complex animations that may obscure the message. **B. Match the Style**: Align the animation style with the overall theme and tone of your video. Consistency is key to maintaining a professional look. **C. Use Easing**: Apply easing to keyframes to create smoother and more natural animations. Use ease-in and ease-out for gradual acceleration and deceleration. **D. Preview and Adjust**: Regularly preview your animations and make necessary adjustments to ensure they appear smooth and polished.

By mastering text animation techniques, you can add a dynamic and engaging element to your video projects, enhancing their visual appeal and storytelling.

CHAPTER 9: EXPORTING AND SHARING YOUR VIDEO

Understanding Export Settings

Getting the export settings right is crucial to ensure your video maintains its quality and plays correctly across different platforms and devices. Here's a detailed guide to help you understand and adjust export settings:

1. Video Format

A. Common Video Formats:

1. **H.264**: A popular format for web and social media due to its high compression efficiency and good quality. Ideal for platforms like YouTube and Vimeo.
2. **MOV**: Often used for professional editing and high-quality exports. It supports a wide range of codecs.
3. **MP4**: Widely supported and versatile, suitable for many devices and platforms.
4. **AVI**: An older format with less compression, resulting in larger file sizes but good quality.
5. **ProRes**: A high-quality codec used in professional workflows, often for post-production and broadcasting.

B. Choosing the Right Format:

- **Web and Social Media**: H.264 (MP4) for its balance of quality and file size.

- **Professional Use**: ProRes or MOV for high-quality exports.
- **Archiving**: Choose a format that preserves the best quality, such as ProRes or Lossless codecs.

2. Resolution and Frame Rate

A. Resolution Settings:

- **1080p (Full HD)**: Standard resolution for most online platforms and high-definition playback.
- **4K (Ultra HD)**: Higher resolution providing more detail and clarity. Ideal for professional projects, streaming services, and future-proofing.
- **720p (HD)**: Lower resolution, often used for quicker uploads and smaller file sizes.

B. Frame Rate Settings:

- **24 fps**: Standard cinematic frame rate, often used to achieve a film-like look.
- **30 fps**: Common frame rate for TV broadcasts, online videos, and general use.
- **60 fps**: Higher frame rate used for smooth motion, ideal for sports, gaming, and action scenes.

C. Aspect Ratio:

- **16:9**: Standard widescreen format for most videos and platforms.
- **4:3**: Classic TV format, less commonly used today.
- **Square (1:1)**: Popular for social media platforms like Instagram.
- **Vertical (9:16)**: Used for mobile videos and platforms like TikTok and Instagram Stories.

3. Bitrate Settings

A. Understanding Bitrate:

- **Bitrate**: The amount of data processed per second in a video file, affecting its quality and file size.

- **Higher Bitrate**: Results in better quality but larger file sizes.
- **Lower Bitrate**: Reduces file size but may sacrifice quality.

B. Choosing the Right Bitrate:

- **Target Bitrate**: Set a target bitrate based on your output needs. For example, 10-15 Mbps for 1080p HD video on YouTube, 25-45 Mbps for 4K video.
- **Maximum Bitrate**: Set a maximum bitrate to control the peak quality and file size.

4. Audio Settings

A. Audio Format:

- **AAC**: Common audio format for web and streaming, offering good quality at lower bitrates.
- **WAV**: Uncompressed format, providing the highest quality but larger file sizes.
- **MP3**: Compressed format, suitable for smaller file sizes at the expense of quality.

B. Bitrate and Sampling Rate:

- **Bitrate**: Choose a bitrate appropriate for your project. For example, 128-256 kbps for AAC audio.
- **Sampling Rate**: Common sampling rates include 44.1 kHz and 48 kHz. Higher sampling rates provide better audio fidelity.

5. Export Presets

A. Using Presets:

- **Export Presets**: Most editing software offers presets for different platforms and use cases (e.g., YouTube, Vimeo, Mobile Devices).
- **Custom Presets**: Save your own presets with preferred settings for repeat use, ensuring consistency across projects.

B. Examples in Popular Software:

1. **Adobe Premiere Pro**:
   - **Presets**: Navigate to the Export Settings window and select from various built-in presets or create custom ones.
   - **Media Encoder**: Use Adobe Media Encoder for batch exports and additional formatting options.
2. **Final Cut Pro**:
   - **Export Options**: Use the Share menu to select presets tailored for different platforms. Save custom export settings for specific needs.
3. **DaVinci Resolve**:
   - **Deliver Page**: Use the Deliver page to access a range of export presets, including options for web, broadcast, and custom settings.

6. Best Practices for Exporting

A. Test Exports: Always run test exports to ensure settings are correct and the final output meets your quality standards. **B. Check Compatibility**: Verify that the exported video plays correctly across different devices and platforms. **C. Archive High-Quality Versions**: Save high-quality versions of your final project for future use or re-edits. **D. Optimize for Web**: Use settings that balance quality and file size for faster uploads and better streaming performance.

By understanding and utilizing proper export settings, you'll ensure that your videos maintain high quality and are optimized for viewing across various platforms and devices.

Choosing the Right Resolution and Bitrate

Selecting the appropriate resolution and bitrate is essential to achieving the best quality for your video while managing file size and compatibility. Here's a detailed guide to help you choose the right settings:

1. Choosing the Right Resolution

A. Common Resolutions:

- **1080p (Full HD)**: 1920x1080 pixels. Ideal for most online platforms and high-definition displays. It strikes a good balance between quality and file size.
- **4K (Ultra HD)**: 3840x2160 pixels. Provides higher detail and clarity, suitable for professional projects, streaming services, and future-proofing content.
- **720p (HD)**: 1280x720 pixels. Used for quicker uploads, smaller file sizes, and older devices that may not support higher resolutions.
- **480p (SD)**: 640x480 pixels. Standard definition, often used for longer videos where file size needs to be minimized.

B. Considerations for Choosing Resolution:

- **Target Platform**: Consider where the video will be viewed. For example, YouTube supports various resolutions, but 1080p and 4K are commonly preferred for high-quality content.
- **Playback Devices**: Think about the devices on which your audience will watch the video. Higher resolutions are beneficial for viewers with high-definition screens.
- **Recording Resolution**: Match the export resolution with the resolution at which the video was recorded to avoid quality loss.

2. Choosing the Right Bitrate

A. Understanding Bitrate:

- **Bitrate**: The amount of data processed per second in a video file. Measured in megabits per second (Mbps) for video and kilobits per second (kbps) for audio.
- **Higher Bitrate**: Results in better quality but larger file sizes.

- **Lower Bitrate**: Reduces file size but may sacrifice quality.

B. Recommended Bitrates for Common Resolutions:

- **1080p (Full HD):**
  - **Standard Quality**: 10-15 Mbps
  - **High Quality**: 20-25 Mbps
- **4K (Ultra HD):**
  - **Standard Quality**: 25-35 Mbps
  - **High Quality**: 40-60 Mbps
- **720p (HD):**
  - **Standard Quality**: 5-10 Mbps
  - **High Quality**: 10-15 Mbps
- **480p (SD):**
  - **Standard Quality**: 2.5-5 Mbps
  - **High Quality**: 5-8 Mbps

3. Balancing Quality and File Size

A. Compression:

- **Goal**: Compress the video to a manageable file size while maintaining acceptable quality.
- **Codec**: Use efficient codecs like H.264 for good compression with minimal quality loss.

B. Factors Affecting Bitrate and Quality:

- **Content Complexity**: Videos with a lot of movement and detail require higher bitrates to maintain quality.
- **Duration**: Longer videos may require lower bitrates to keep file sizes reasonable.

C. Adjusting Bitrate in Software:

1. **Adobe Premiere Pro**:
   - **Bitrate Settings**: In the Export Settings window, adjust the target and maximum bitrate sliders.
   - **Variable Bitrate (VBR)**: Use VBR for better

quality at variable data rates, allowing for lower file sizes without compromising quality.

2. **Final Cut Pro**:
   ◦ **Bitrate Adjustment**: Use the Share menu to access export settings and adjust the bitrate manually.
   ◦ **Preset Options**: Select from preset options that balance quality and file size for different platforms.

3. **DaVinci Resolve**:
   ◦ **Deliver Page**: Set the bitrate under the Video tab in the Deliver page. Choose between constant bitrate (CBR) or variable bitrate (VBR) settings.

4. Best Practices for Resolution and Bitrate

A. Test and Preview: Always run test exports to ensure the chosen settings deliver the desired quality. **B. Adjust Based on Feedback**: Be prepared to adjust the resolution or bitrate based on playback quality and feedback from viewers. **C. Optimize for Specific Platforms**: Follow platform-specific guidelines for resolutions and bitrates to ensure optimal performance (e.g., YouTube, Vimeo, social media platforms). **D. Balance Quality and File Size**: Aim for a balance between high quality and manageable file sizes to ensure easy sharing and playback.

By carefully selecting the appropriate resolution and bitrate, you can ensure your videos look great across various platforms and devices while maintaining reasonable file sizes.

Exporting for Different Platforms (YouTube, Vimeo, Social Media)

Each platform has its specific requirements and recommendations for video exports. Ensuring your video meets these standards will help maintain quality and playback compatibility. Here's a detailed guide to exporting for YouTube,

Vimeo, and social media:

1. Exporting for YouTube

A. Recommended Settings:

- **Format**: MP4 (H.264)
- **Resolution**:
  - 4K (3840x2160)
  - 1080p (1920x1080)
  - 720p (1280x720)
- **Frame Rate**:
  - 24 fps (standard cinematic)
  - 30 fps (general use)
  - 60 fps (smooth motion)
- **Bitrate**:
  - 1080p: 8-12 Mbps for standard HD
  - 4K: 30-60 Mbps for UHD content

B. Steps to Export:

1. **Adobe Premiere Pro**:
   - **Export Settings**: Go to File > Export > Media. In the Export Settings window, choose H.264 format and select the YouTube 1080p or 4K preset.
   - **Customize Bitrate**: Adjust the bitrate settings under the Video tab to meet YouTube's recommendations.

2. **Final Cut Pro**:
   - **Share Menu**: Go to the Share menu and select YouTube & Facebook. Customize the resolution and format as needed.

3. **DaVinci Resolve**:
   - **Deliver Page**: In the Deliver page, use the YouTube preset and customize the settings for

resolution and bitrate.

2. Exporting for Vimeo

A. Recommended Settings:

- **Format**: MP4 (H.264)
- **Resolution**:
  - 4K (3840x2160)
  - 1080p (1920x1080)
  - 720p (1280x720)
- **Frame Rate**:
  - 24 fps
  - 30 fps
  - 60 fps
- **Bitrate**:
  - 1080p: 10-15 Mbps
  - 4K: 50-60 Mbps

B. Steps to Export:

1. **Adobe Premiere Pro**:
   - **Export Settings**: Go to File > Export > Media. Choose H.264 format and select the Vimeo 1080p or 4K preset.
   - **Customize Bitrate**: Adjust bitrate settings under the Video tab to match Vimeo's recommendations.

2. **Final Cut Pro**:
   - **Share Menu**: Go to the Share menu and select Vimeo. Customize the resolution and format as needed.

3. **DaVinci Resolve**:
   - **Deliver Page**: In the Deliver page, use the Vimeo preset and customize the settings for resolution and bitrate.

3. Exporting for Social Media (Instagram, Facebook, Twitter)
A. Recommended Settings:
Instagram:

- **Format:** MP4 (H.264)
- **Resolution:**
  - Square (1080x1080)
  - Vertical (1080x1350)
  - Stories (1080x1920)
- **Frame Rate:** 30 fps
- **Bitrate:** 5-8 Mbps

Facebook:

- **Format:** MP4 (H.264)
- **Resolution:**
  - 1080p (1920x1080)
  - 720p (1280x720)
- **Frame Rate:** 30 fps
- **Bitrate:** 5-10 Mbps

Twitter:

- **Format:** MP4 (H.264)
- **Resolution:**
  - 1080p (1920x1080)
  - 720p (1280x720)
- **Frame Rate:** 30 fps
- **Bitrate:** 5-10 Mbps

B. Steps to Export:
1. **Adobe Premiere Pro:**
   - **Export Settings:** Go to File > Export > Media. Choose H.264 format and select a social media preset (e.g., Instagram, Facebook).
   - **Customize Resolution:** Adjust resolution

settings to match the platform's recommendations.

2. **Final Cut Pro**:

   ◦ **Share Menu**: Go to the Share menu and select the appropriate social media option. Customize the resolution and format as needed.

3. **DaVinci Resolve**:

   ◦ **Deliver Page**: In the Deliver page, use a social media preset and customize the settings for resolution and bitrate.

4. General Tips for Exporting

A. Aspect Ratio: Ensure the aspect ratio matches the platform's requirements to avoid cropping or black bars. **B. File Size**: Balance quality and file size to ensure quick uploads and smooth playback. **C. Preview Exports**: Always preview your exports to make sure they look and sound good on the intended platform. **D. Optimize for Mobile**: Consider optimizing exports for mobile viewing, especially for social media platforms.

By following these guidelines, you can ensure your videos are optimized for the best quality and performance across different platforms.

Backup and Archiving Strategies

To protect your video projects from data loss and ensure their longevity, it is essential to implement effective backup and archiving strategies. Here's a detailed guide to help you secure your valuable work:

1. Understanding Backup and Archiving

A. Backup vs. Archiving:

   • **Backup**: Creating copies of your files to protect against accidental loss, corruption, or hardware failure. Backups are typically updated regularly.

   • **Archiving**: Long-term storage of your completed

projects and important files. Archives are more static and used to preserve project versions for future reference.

2. Backup Strategies

A. Types of Backups:

1. **Full Backup**: A complete copy of all your data. It is comprehensive but can take up significant storage space.

2. **Incremental Backup**: Only backs up changes made since the last backup, saving storage space and time compared to a full backup.

3. **Differential Backup**: Backs up all changes made since the last full backup. Requires more storage than incremental but is quicker to restore.

B. Creating a Backup Plan:

1. **3-2-1 Rule**: Store at least three copies of your data (one primary and two backups) on two different media types, with one copy offsite.

2. **Regular Schedule**: Establish a regular backup schedule (e.g., daily, weekly) to ensure your data is consistently protected.

3. **Automated Backups**: Use backup software to automate the backup process, reducing the risk of human error.

C. Storing Backups:

1. **Local Backups**: Store backups on external hard drives, NAS (Network Attached Storage) devices, or other local media.

2. **Offsite Backups**: Keep a copy of your backup in a different physical location to protect against site-specific incidents like fire or theft.

3. **Cloud Backups**: Utilize cloud storage services for offsite backups. Providers like Google Drive, Dropbox, and Microsoft OneDrive offer reliable options.

3. Archiving Strategies

A. Organizing Archives:

1. **Project-Based Organization**: Archive files by project, keeping all related assets (e.g., media, documents, project files) together.

2. **Version Control**: Maintain versions of your projects to track changes and revert to previous states if needed.

3. **Metadata and Documentation**: Include metadata and documentation with your archives to provide context, making it easier to understand and retrieve files in the future.

B. Choosing Archival Storage:

1. **External Hard Drives**: Suitable for large volumes of data, but ensure drives are stored in a safe environment to prevent damage.

2. **Optical Media**: DVDs and Blu-rays offer long-term storage but have limited capacity and slower access speeds.

3. **Tape Storage**: Ideal for very large archives, providing high capacity and durability, though access can be slow.

4. **Cloud Storage**: Reliable and scalable, but consider the cost and ensure security measures are in place.

C. Archiving Workflow:

1. **Consolidate Assets**: Gather all project files, including raw footage, edited sequences, graphics, and audio.

2. **Create an Archive**: Use archival software or manual processes to create a structured archive.

3. **Verify Archive**: Ensure all files are correctly archived and accessible. Perform regular audits to check the integrity of archived data.

4. Best Practices for Backup and Archiving

A. Redundancy: Always have multiple backups and archives to safeguard against data loss. **B. Regular Updates**: Keep your backup and archival plans up to date with the latest project files and versions. **C. Security**: Implement security measures to protect your data, especially when using cloud storage or offsite backups. **D. Documentation**: Maintain detailed documentation of your backup and archiving procedures to ensure they are followed correctly. **E. Testing**: Regularly test your backups and archives to ensure they can be successfully restored when needed.

By implementing these backup and archiving strategies, you can protect your video projects from data loss and ensure their preservation for future use.

CHAPTER 10: SPECIAL PROJECT: CREATING A SHORT FILM

Pre-Production Planning

Pre-production is the foundation of any successful short film project. Proper planning and organization ensure that your production runs smoothly and efficiently. Here's a detailed guide to help you navigate the pre-production phase:

1. Developing the Concept

A. Idea Generation:

- **Brainstorming**: Generate various ideas and select the most compelling one. Consider themes, genres, and messages you want to convey.
- **Research**: Gather inspiration from other films, books, or real-life events. Research the feasibility of your ideas.

B. Writing the Script:

- **Outline**: Create a detailed outline of your story, including key plot points and character arcs.
- **Scriptwriting**: Write the screenplay, ensuring it follows the standard script format. Focus on dialogue, action, and scene descriptions.
- **Revisions**: Revise and edit the script based on feedback from peers or mentors.

2. Planning the Production

A. Creating a Storyboard:

- **Visualizing Scenes**: Draw or use software to create a series of frames that represent each scene. Include notes on camera angles, movements, and key actions.
- **Shot List**: Develop a comprehensive shot list based on the storyboard, detailing all the shots you need to capture.

B. Budgeting:

- **Estimate Costs**: Develop a budget that includes costs for equipment, locations, talent, crew, props, costumes, and post-production.
- **Funding**: Explore funding options such as personal savings, crowdfunding, grants, or sponsorships.

C. Scheduling:

- **Production Schedule**: Create a detailed production schedule that outlines all the tasks and deadlines. Use tools like production calendars and project management software.
- **Call Sheets**: Prepare call sheets for each day of the shoot, detailing crew call times, locations, and scene information.

3. Assembling the Team

A. Key Crew Members:

- **Director**: Oversees the creative vision and guides the cast and crew.
- **Producer**: Manages the logistics, budget, and overall production.
- **Cinematographer**: Handles the camera work and visual style.
- **Sound Designer**: Manages audio recording and sound effects.
- **Editor**: Assembles the footage and handles post-

production.

B. Casting:

- **Auditions**: Hold auditions to select the best actors for each role. Consider the chemistry between actors and their ability to bring characters to life.
- **Talent Agreements**: Draft and sign contracts with your actors, outlining the terms of their involvement.

4. Securing Locations and Permits

A. Scouting Locations:

- **Finding the Right Spots**: Identify potential locations that fit your script's requirements. Consider factors such as accessibility, lighting, and noise levels.
- **Location Photos**: Take photos or videos of each location to help plan your shots and visualize the scenes.

B. Obtaining Permits:

- **Permissions**: Obtain necessary permissions or permits from property owners, local authorities, or governing bodies to film at your chosen locations.
- **Insurance**: Secure production insurance to cover potential accidents, damages, or liabilities during the shoot.

5. Preparing Equipment and Props

A. Equipment List:

- **Camera Gear**: Ensure you have all the necessary camera equipment, including cameras, lenses, tripods, and stabilizers.
- **Audio Gear**: Gather microphones, audio recorders, and boom poles for capturing high-quality sound.
- **Lighting Gear**: Include lights, reflectors, and diffusers to achieve proper illumination.

B. Props and Costumes:

- **Prop List**: Create a list of all props needed for each scene.

Source or create these props ahead of time.

- **Costumes**: Design and acquire costumes that fit the characters and setting. Ensure actors have their costumes prior to filming.

6. Rehearsals and Preparations

A. Script Read-Through:

- **Cast Reading**: Organize a cast read-through of the script to familiarize everyone with their lines and the story.

B. Blocking and Rehearsals:

- **Blocking**: Plan and rehearse the actors' movements within each scene. Ensure that blocking matches the storyboard and shot list.
- **On-Set Rehearsals**: Conduct rehearsals at the actual locations to help actors and crew get comfortable with the space and flow of the scenes.

7. Final Preparations

A. Checklist:

- **Final Check**: Go through a comprehensive checklist to ensure all elements are in place before the shoot, including equipment, props, costumes, and permits.
- **Backup Plans**: Prepare contingency plans for potential issues such as weather changes, equipment failures, or scheduling conflicts.

By meticulously planning the pre-production phase, you set the stage for a successful and smooth filming process.

Scripting and Storyboarding

Scripting and storyboarding are crucial steps in the pre-production phase of creating a short film. They provide a clear blueprint for your film and ensure that everyone on your team shares the same vision. Here's a detailed guide to help you with scripting and storyboarding:

1. Scripting

A. Developing the Script:

1. **Idea Generation**: Start with a compelling idea. Think about the story you want to tell and its core message.

2. **Outline**: Create a detailed outline of your story, breaking it down into key scenes and plot points.

3. **Screenplay Format**: Write your script in standard screenplay format, which includes scene headings, action lines, character names, dialogue, and transitions.

B. Script Components:

1. **Scene Headings**: Also known as sluglines, these indicate the location and time of each scene (e.g., INT. COFFEE SHOP – DAY).

2. **Action Lines**: Describe the events happening in the scene. Keep these concise and vivid.

3. **Character Names**: Write character names in uppercase the first time they appear and when they speak.

4. **Dialogue**: Write the dialogue for each character, ensuring it sounds natural and conveys the intended emotion.

5. **Parentheticals**: Provide brief instructions on how the dialogue should be delivered (e.g., [sarcastically]).

6. **Transitions**: Indicate how one scene transitions to another (e.g., CUT TO:, FADE IN:).

C. Revising the Script:

1. **Feedback**: Share your script with trusted peers, mentors, or colleagues for constructive feedback.

2. **Revisions**: Incorporate feedback and revise your script to improve clarity, pacing, and emotional impact.

2. Storyboarding

A. Purpose of Storyboarding:

- **Visual Representation**: Storyboards provide a visual representation of each scene, helping to plan camera angles, movements, and compositions.

. **Communication Tool**: They serve as a communication tool for the director, cinematographer, and crew, ensuring everyone understands the visual plan.

B. Creating a Storyboard:

1. **Draw or Use Software**: Create storyboards by drawing frames manually or using software like Storyboard That, Toon Boom Storyboard Pro, or Adobe Illustrator.

2. **Frames**: Each frame represents a key shot or moment in the scene. Include notes on camera angles, movements, and important actions.

3. **Sequence**: Arrange frames in sequence to visualize the flow of the film.

C. Components of a Storyboard:

1. **Scene Description**: Include a brief description of the scene and action happening in each frame.

2. **Camera Directions**: Note the camera angles, movements, and transitions (e.g., close-up, pan, tilt).

3. **Dialogue and Sound**: Add any important dialogue or sound effects that correspond to the visuals.

3. Combining Script and Storyboard

A. Alignment:

. **Consistency**: Ensure your storyboard aligns with your script. The visual plan should accurately reflect the story and dialogue in the screenplay.

. **Revisions**: Be open to revising the script or storyboard if needed to improve clarity and coherence.

B. Integration:

. **Shot List**: Use the storyboard to create a detailed shot list, specifying every shot that needs to be captured during production.

. **Production Plan**: Integrate the script and storyboard

into your overall production plan, ensuring all elements are coordinated and prepared for filming.

4. Best Practices

A. Detailed Planning: Spend ample time planning and refining your script and storyboard. This preparation will save time and effort during production and post-production. **B. Collaboration**: Work closely with your team, including the director, cinematographer, and actors, to ensure everyone understands and buys into the vision. **C. Flexibility**: While it's important to have a clear plan, remain flexible and open to creative changes that may arise during filming. **D. Visualization Tools**: Use visualization tools like concept art, location photos, and reference videos to complement your storyboards and scripts.

By thoroughly scripting and storyboarding your short film, you lay a strong foundation for a successful production.

Shooting and Directing

The shooting and directing phase is where your vision truly comes to life. Here's a detailed guide on how to effectively manage the shooting process and direct your short film:

1. Preparing for the Shoot

A. Finalizing the Plan:

1. **Shot List**: Have a detailed shot list ready, based on your storyboard. This ensures you capture all necessary shots and stay organized.

2. **Call Sheets**: Distribute call sheets to the cast and crew, outlining the schedule, locations, and contact information for each shooting day.

3. **Rehearsals**: Conduct rehearsals to ensure that everyone knows their roles and the scenes flow smoothly.

B. Equipment Check:

1. **Camera Gear**: Ensure all camera equipment is ready, including cameras, lenses, tripods, and stabilizers.

2. **Audio Gear**: Test microphones, audio recorders, and boom poles to capture high-quality sound.

3. **Lighting Gear**: Set up lights, reflectors, and diffusers to achieve proper illumination for each scene.

2. Directing the Shoot

A. Working with Actors:

1. **Communicate Clearly**: Provide clear and concise direction to your actors. Ensure they understand their motivations and emotions for each scene.

2. **Encourage Feedback**: Foster an open environment where actors can provide input and ask questions.

3. **Rehearse on Set**: Conduct brief rehearsals on location to help actors get comfortable with the set and block their movements.

B. Managing the Crew:

1. **Assign Roles**: Make sure each crew member knows their responsibilities, from camera operators to sound technicians.

2. **Foster Teamwork**: Encourage collaboration and support among the crew to maintain a positive and efficient working environment.

3. **Stay Organized**: Keep the set organized and ensure that all equipment is accounted for and properly handled.

C. Capturing the Shots:

1. **Follow the Storyboard**: Use the storyboard as a guide to frame and compose each shot. Ensure each scene is captured from the planned angles.

2. **Check Sound Levels**: Monitor audio levels to avoid distortion or background noise. Ensure all dialogue and sound effects are clear.

3. **Review Footage**: Regularly review footage on set to ensure it meets your expectations and make

adjustments as necessary.

3. Handling Challenges on Set

A. Adapting to Changes:

1. **Flexible Planning**: Be prepared to adapt to unforeseen challenges, such as changes in weather, location issues, or equipment malfunctions.

2. **Problem Solving**: Think creatively to find solutions to unexpected problems. Stay calm and resourceful.

B. Managing Time:

1. **Stay on Schedule**: Keep track of time and ensure that each scene is completed within the planned time frame.

2. **Prioritize Shots**: If you're running behind, prioritize essential shots and adjust the schedule accordingly.

C. Maintaining Energy:

1. **Encourage Breaks**: Ensure the cast and crew take regular breaks to stay energized and focused.

2. **Positive Atmosphere**: Maintain a positive and encouraging atmosphere to keep morale high and the team motivated.

4. Directing Techniques

A. Shot Composition:

1. **Rule of Thirds**: Use the rule of thirds to create balanced and visually appealing compositions.

2. **Leading Lines**: Utilize leading lines to guide the viewer's eye through the frame.

3. **Framing**: Frame your shots to convey the desired mood and focus on the subject.

B. Camera Movement:

1. **Static Shots**: Use static shots for stability and focus in dialogue-heavy scenes.

2. **Panning and Tilting**: Employ panning and tilting for dynamic movement and to follow the action.

3. **Tracking Shots**: Use tracking shots to create smooth movement and immerse the audience in the scene.

C. Lighting Techniques:

1. **Three-Point Lighting**: Use three-point lighting (key light, fill light, back light) for professional and balanced illumination.
2. **Natural Light**: Take advantage of natural light and adjust your settings accordingly to avoid overexposure or shadows.
3. **Creative Lighting**: Experiment with lighting setups to create mood and atmosphere, such as using colored gels or practical lights.

5. Best Practices for Shooting and Directing

A. Be Prepared: Thorough preparation and planning are key to a successful shoot. Ensure all elements are in place before you begin. **B. Stay Flexible**: Adaptability is crucial. Be ready to adjust your plans based on real-time challenges and opportunities. **C. Communicate Effectively**: Clear communication with your cast and crew is essential for a smooth production. Ensure everyone understands their roles and responsibilities. **D. Monitor Continuity**: Pay attention to continuity details, such as props, costumes, and actor positions, to ensure consistency across scenes. **E. Enjoy the Process**: Filmmaking can be challenging, but it's also a creative and rewarding experience. Enjoy the process and foster a collaborative atmosphere on set.

By effectively managing the shooting process and directing your short film, you can bring your vision to life and create a compelling and well-crafted final product.

Final Editing and Post-Production

Once the shooting phase is complete, the next crucial step is the final editing and post-production process. This stage involves assembling your footage, applying visual and audio enhancements, and ensuring the film flows seamlessly. Here's a detailed guide:

1. Organizing Footage

A. Importing Media:

1. **Gathering Clips**: Import all your recorded footage into your editing software. Organize clips into bins or folders based on scenes, takes, or shot types.

2. **Backing Up**: Ensure all media files are backed up in multiple locations to prevent data loss.

B. Reviewing and Selecting:

1. **Watch Through**: View all your footage to identify the best takes and note any standout performances or shots.

2. **Marking**: Use markers or tags to label good takes and organize them for easy access during the editing process.

2. Assembling the Rough Cut

A. Timeline Assembly:

1. **Import Clips**: Place your selected clips onto the editing timeline in the order of your story.

2. **Trim and Adjust**: Trim clips to the desired length and adjust their placement to create a coherent sequence.

B. Creating the Flow:

1. **Transitions**: Use transitions like cuts, dissolves, and fades to ensure smooth visual flow between clips.

2. **Pacing**: Adjust the pacing of your film by varying the length of clips and transitions to match the desired rhythm and mood.

3. Fine-Tuning the Edit

A. Cutting for Precision:

1. **Tightening Scenes**: Remove any unnecessary footage or pauses to tighten the scene and maintain engagement.

2. **Frame Accuracy**: Make frame-accurate cuts to ensure precise timing of actions and dialogue.

B. Enhancing Visuals:

1. **Color Correction**: Apply color correction to ensure consistent and natural-looking colors throughout the film.
2. **Color Grading**: Use color grading to create a specific mood or visual style that enhances the story's emotional impact.
3. **Stabilization**: Use stabilization tools to smooth out shaky footage.

C. Adding Effects:

1. **Visual Effects (VFX)**: Incorporate visual effects as needed, such as green screen compositions, CGI elements, or motion graphics.
2. **Text and Graphics**: Add titles, lower thirds, and any necessary graphics to provide information and enhance visual appeal.

4. Working on Audio

A. Syncing Audio:

1. **Aligning Dialogue**: Ensure all dialogue is synced correctly with the video footage.
2. **Using Waveforms**: Utilize audio waveforms to match visual cues with corresponding sound.

B. Audio Editing:

1. **Sound Design**: Add sound effects, ambient sounds, and Foley to create a rich audio environment.
2. **Noise Reduction**: Remove background noise and unwanted sounds using noise reduction filters.
3. **EQ and Compression**: Apply equalization (EQ) and compression to balance audio levels and enhance clarity.

C. Audio Mixing:

1. **Balancing Levels**: Ensure all audio elements (dialogue, music, sound effects) are balanced and clearly audible.

2. **Panning and Spatial Effects**: Use panning to place audio elements within the stereo field for a more immersive experience.

3. **Mastering**: Apply final mastering techniques to ensure a polished and professional sound.

5. Final Touches

A. Reviewing and Polishing:

1. **Watch Through**: Conduct multiple watch-throughs to catch any remaining errors or areas for improvement.

2. **Feedback**: Share the rough cut with trusted peers or mentors for feedback and make necessary adjustments.

B. Exporting the Film:

1. **Export Settings**: Choose the appropriate export settings based on your intended platform (e.g., YouTube, Vimeo, film festivals).

2. **Multiple Versions**: Export multiple versions of your film, including high-quality master files for archiving and compressed versions for online sharing.

6. Best Practices for Editing and Post-Production

A. Stay Organized: Keep your project files and assets well-organized to streamline the editing process. **B. Use Shortcuts**: Learn and use keyboard shortcuts to speed up your workflow. **C. Regularly Save**: Save your work frequently and create backup copies to prevent data loss. **D. Maintain Consistency**: Ensure that visual and audio elements are consistent throughout the film to create a cohesive final product. **E. Enjoy the Process**: Editing and post-production can be a creative and rewarding stage. Take your time to craft a film that you're proud of.

By following these steps, you can bring your short film to its final polished form, ready to be shared with the world.

CHAPTER 11: TRENDS AND INNOVATIONS IN VIDEO EDITING

AI in Video Editing

Artificial Intelligence (AI) is revolutionizing video editing, bringing advanced technology to streamline workflows, enhance creativity, and make the editing process more efficient. Here's a detailed exploration of how AI is shaping the future of video editing:

1. AI-Powered Automation

A. Automated Editing: AI algorithms can automatically analyze footage, identify key scenes, and suggest edits. This reduces the time editors spend on manual tasks, allowing them to focus more on the creative aspects1. For example, AI can handle tasks like cutting and arranging clips, creating rough cuts, and even adding transitions.

B. Real-Time Editing: With advancements in AI processing power, real-time video editing is becoming a reality. Editors can see the effects of their edits instantly without waiting for rendering times2. This significantly speeds up the workflow and allows for immediate creative decisions.

2. AI-Driven Storytelling

A. Content Analysis: AI can analyze the content and context of footage to suggest the best way to tell a story. This includes recommending scene transitions, pacing, and emotional tone to craft compelling narratives that resonate with audiences2.

B. Predictive Tools: AI tools can predict editors' actions based on previous editing patterns and preferences. These tools streamline the editing process by offering suggestions such as applying specific filters or transitions, enhancing productivity2.

3. Enhancing Visual and Audio Quality

A. Color Correction and Grading: AI-powered tools can automatically perform color correction and grading, ensuring consistent visual quality throughout the video. These tools can also recognize different lighting conditions and adjust colors to achieve the desired look.

B. Noise Reduction and Audio Enhancement: AI can reduce background noise and enhance audio quality. This is particularly useful for improving dialogue clarity and overall sound quality in videos.

4. Streamlining Collaboration

A. Cloud-Based Editing: AI integration with cloud-based platforms allows editors to collaborate on the same project from different locations in real-time. This streamlines workflows and reduces delays, making remote collaboration seamless1.

B. AI-Avatars and Voiceovers: AI-generated avatars and voiceovers are transforming how presenters and characters are incorporated into videos, providing cost-effective and highly customizable digital personas.

5. Innovations in Video Formats

A. Text-to-Video Generation: AI models can create videos based on written scripts, enabling rapid content production without traditional filming. This is particularly useful for creating explainer videos, tutorials, and promotional content.

B. Virtual Reality (VR) and Augmented Reality (AR): AI is enhancing immersive experiences with VR and AR, allowing creators to craft interactive and engaging videos. AI can also assist in editing 360-degree videos for a more interactive viewing experience1.

6. Data-Driven Insights

A. Video Analytics: AI-driven video analytics provide detailed insights into viewer behavior and preferences. By analyzing data such as watch time, drop-off points, and engagement rates, creators can optimize their videos for better performance2.

B. Integration with Social Media: AI tools can analyze social media trends and user engagement to help creators tailor their content to specific platforms5. This ensures that videos resonate with the target audience and achieve maximum reach.

By leveraging AI in video editing, editors can enhance their creativity, efficiency, and the overall quality of their projects.

Virtual Reality and 360-Degree Video

Virtual Reality (VR) and 360-degree video are revolutionizing the way we create and experience content. These technologies offer immersive experiences that engage viewers in entirely new ways. Here's a comprehensive guide to understanding and implementing VR and 360-degree video in your projects:

1. Understanding VR and 360-Degree Video

A. Virtual Reality (VR):

- **Definition**: VR is an immersive technology that creates a simulated environment, allowing users to interact with the surroundings using VR headsets and controllers.
- **Applications**: Used in gaming, simulations, training, healthcare, education, and entertainment.

B. 360-Degree Video:

- **Definition**: 360-degree video captures a panoramic view of the scene, allowing viewers to look in all directions as if they were present in the environment.
- **Applications**: Popular in virtual tours, documentaries, concerts, sports, and immersive storytelling.

2. Equipment and Tools

A. Cameras:

1. **360-Degree Cameras**: Designed specifically for capturing panoramic video. Examples include the GoPro MAX, Insta360, and Ricoh Theta.

2. **VR Cameras**: Offer higher quality and more immersive VR content. Examples include the RED Komodo and Z CAM V1 Pro.

B. Editing Software:

1. **Adobe Premiere Pro**: Offers tools for editing 360-degree video, including VR Effects and VR Transitions.

2. **Final Cut Pro**: Provides 360-degree editing capabilities with effects and titles designed for immersive content.

3. **DaVinci Resolve**: Supports 360-degree video editing and VR workflows with Fusion for advanced compositing.

4. **Adobe After Effects**: Ideal for creating and enhancing VR content with advanced visual effects and motion graphics.

3. Capturing 360-Degree Video

A. Camera Setup:

1. **Mounting and Stabilization**: Use stabilizers and proper mounting techniques to ensure smooth and steady footage.

2. **Positioning**: Place the camera at the center of the action to capture a complete view. Avoid placing the camera too close to subjects to reduce distortion.

B. Shooting Techniques:

1. **Plan Your Shots**: Consider the viewer's perspective and plan shots that take advantage of the 360-degree field of view.

2. **Minimize Movement**: Excessive camera movement can cause disorientation. Use slow and deliberate movements to create a comfortable viewing experience.

3. **Avoiding Stitching Issues**: Ensure consistent lighting and avoid overlapping objects that can cause stitching artifacts.

4. Editing 360-Degree Video

A. Importing and Organizing:

1. **Import Footage**: Import 360-degree footage into your editing software and organize it into bins or folders.

2. **Stitching**: Use software to stitch together the footage from multiple camera lenses. Some cameras have in-built stitching capabilities.

B. Applying Effects and Transitions:

1. **VR Effects**: Apply VR effects designed for 360-degree content, such as VR blurs or VR color corrections.

2. **VR Transitions**: Use VR transitions to create smooth and immersive transitions between scenes.

C. Exporting:

1. **Export Settings**: Choose export settings optimized for 360-degree video, ensuring compatibility with VR platforms.

2. **Metadata**: Add 360-degree metadata to the video file to ensure proper display on platforms like YouTube and Facebook.

5. Best Practices for VR and 360-Degree Video

A. Storytelling Techniques:

1. **Engage the Viewer**: Create interactive and engaging content that takes advantage of the immersive nature of VR and 360-degree video.

2. **Direct Attention**: Use visual cues, audio, and movement to guide the viewer's attention to important parts of the scene.

B. Technical Considerations:

1. **Resolution**: Shoot at the highest possible resolution to

ensure clarity and detail in the final VR experience.

2. **Frame Rate**: Use higher frame rates (e.g., 60 fps) for smoother motion and a more comfortable viewing experience.

C. Viewer Experience:

1. **Accessibility**: Ensure your content is accessible on various VR platforms and devices.

2. **Testing**: Test your VR and 360-degree videos on different VR headsets to ensure they provide the intended experience.

By embracing VR and 360-degree video, you can create immersive and engaging content that captivates your audience and offers a unique viewing experience.

Collaborative Editing in the Cloud

Collaborative editing in the cloud has revolutionized the way teams work on video projects, enabling seamless collaboration regardless of geographical locations. Here's a detailed guide to help you understand and implement cloud-based collaborative editing:

1. Benefits of Cloud-Based Collaborative Editing

A. Real-Time Collaboration:

- **Teamwork**: Multiple editors, designers, and producers can work on the same project simultaneously. This increases efficiency and fosters better teamwork.
- **Instant Feedback**: Team members can give and receive feedback in real-time, allowing for quicker decision-making and workflow adjustments.

B. Accessibility:

- **Remote Access**: Editors can access projects from anywhere with an internet connection, eliminating the need for physical presence.
- **Device Flexibility**: Cloud-based platforms allow you to

work from various devices, including desktops, laptops, and even tablets.

C. Security and Backup:

- **Data Security**: Cloud services typically provide robust security measures to protect your data.
- **Automatic Backup**: Cloud platforms often include automatic backup features, reducing the risk of data loss.

2. Popular Cloud-Based Editing Platforms

A. Adobe Creative Cloud:

- **Adobe Premiere Pro**: Integrated with Creative Cloud, allowing team members to share projects and assets seamlessly.
- **Team Projects**: Enables real-time collaboration with version control and conflict resolution features.

B. Frame.io:

- **Video Review and Collaboration**: Offers tools for reviewing, commenting, and collaborating on video projects. Integrates with major editing software like Adobe Premiere Pro and Final Cut Pro.

C. Blackmagic Cloud (DaVinci Resolve):

- **Collaboration Features**: DaVinci Resolve offers robust collaboration tools within its software, including multi-user timelines and real-time updates.
- **Cloud Integration**: Supports cloud-based project sharing and collaboration through Blackmagic Cloud.

D. Avid MediaCentral:

- **Centralized Collaboration**: Avid's cloud platform supports collaborative workflows with media management, version control, and secure access to projects.

3. Implementing Collaborative Editing

A. Setting Up Projects:

1. **Create a Centralized Project**: Set up a project in your chosen cloud-based platform, ensuring all team members have access.

2. **Organize Assets**: Store all media assets, graphics, and project files in a structured and easily accessible manner.

B. Assigning Roles and Permissions:

1. **User Roles**: Define roles and permissions for each team member based on their responsibilities (e.g., editor, sound designer, producer).

2. **Access Control**: Ensure that only authorized personnel have access to critical files and project settings.

C. Workflow Management:

1. **Task Assignment**: Use project management tools to assign tasks and track progress. This ensures everyone knows their responsibilities and deadlines.

2. **Version Control**: Maintain version control to track changes and revert to previous versions if needed. Avoid conflicts by clearly communicating edits and updates.

4. Best Practices for Cloud-Based Collaboration

A. Effective Communication:

1. **Regular Meetings**: Schedule regular video calls or meetings to discuss progress, address issues, and provide feedback.

2. **Communication Tools**: Use communication tools like Slack or Microsoft Teams to stay connected and share updates.

B. Efficient Workflow:

1. **Standardize Processes**: Establish standardized workflows and naming conventions to ensure consistency across the project.

2. **Documentation**: Maintain detailed documentation of

editing decisions, feedback, and changes to keep everyone informed.

C. Ensuring Data Security:

1. **Secure Connections**: Always use secure internet connections when accessing cloud-based projects.

2. **Regular Backups**: Ensure that regular backups are being made and that data is stored securely in the cloud.

5. Overcoming Challenges

A. Internet Connectivity:

- **Stable Connection**: Ensure a stable and fast internet connection to avoid disruptions during collaboration.

- **Offline Editing**: Some platforms allow offline editing with synchronization when the connection is restored. Use this feature to maintain productivity.

B. Learning Curve:

- **Training**: Provide training for team members unfamiliar with cloud-based editing tools. This helps ensure a smooth transition and efficient workflow.

By leveraging cloud-based collaborative editing, you can enhance your team's productivity, streamline workflows, and deliver high-quality video projects, even when working from different locations.

Future-Proofing Your Skills

The video editing landscape is constantly evolving, and staying ahead of the curve requires continuous learning and adaptation. Here are some strategies and tips to help you future-proof your video editing skills:

1. Embrace Lifelong Learning

A. Online Courses and Tutorials:

1. **Platforms**: Utilize online learning platforms like Coursera, Udemy, LinkedIn Learning, and Skillshare to access courses taught by industry professionals.

2. **YouTube Channels**: Follow reputable YouTube channels that offer free tutorials and tips on the latest editing techniques and software updates.

B. Certifications:

1. **Adobe Certified Professional**: Obtaining certifications such as the Adobe Certified Professional can validate your skills and enhance your credibility.

2. **Other Certifications**: Consider certifications from platforms like DaVinci Resolve and Avid Media Composer to broaden your expertise.

2. Stay Updated with Technology

A. Software Updates:

1. **Regular Upgrades**: Ensure your editing software is always up-to-date to take advantage of new features, bug fixes, and performance improvements.

2. **Beta Programs**: Join beta programs for early access to upcoming features and provide feedback to developers.

B. Hardware Advancements:

1. **Upgrade Equipment**: Invest in high-performance hardware, such as powerful CPUs, GPUs, and SSDs, to handle demanding editing tasks and improve workflow efficiency.

2. **VR and AR Equipment**: Explore virtual reality (VR) and augmented reality (AR) equipment to stay ahead in immersive content creation.

3. Explore Emerging Trends

A. AI and Machine Learning:

1. **AI-Powered Tools**: Familiarize yourself with AI-powered editing tools that automate repetitive tasks, enhance visual and audio quality, and offer creative suggestions.

2. **Machine Learning**: Understand how machine learning

can be applied to predictive editing and adaptive content creation.

B. 360-Degree and VR Video:

1. **Immersive Content**: Learn to create and edit 360-degree videos and VR content to offer immersive experiences to your audience.
2. **Interactive Storytelling**: Experiment with interactive storytelling techniques that utilize these technologies to engage viewers more deeply.

4. Network and Collaborate

A. Join Professional Communities:

1. **Forums and Groups**: Engage with online forums, social media groups, and professional organizations to connect with other video editors and share knowledge.
2. **Networking Events**: Attend industry events, workshops, and conferences to stay informed about the latest trends and network with peers.

B. Collaborative Projects:

1. **Team Collaborations**: Participate in collaborative projects to gain new perspectives and learn from others' expertise.
2. **Crowdsourcing Platforms**: Utilize crowdsourcing platforms to collaborate with freelancers and creators worldwide.

5. Develop a Diverse Skill Set

A. Broaden Your Expertise:

1. **Software Proficiency**: Gain proficiency in multiple editing software platforms to increase your versatility and adaptability.
2. **Complementary Skills**: Develop complementary skills, such as color grading, sound design, motion graphics, and visual effects, to enhance your value as an editor.

B. Stay Creative:

1. **Experimentation**: Experiment with new techniques, styles, and approaches to push your creative boundaries.

2. **Inspiration**: Draw inspiration from various sources, including films, art, music, and literature, to enrich your creative vision.

By continuously learning, staying updated with technology, exploring emerging trends, networking, and developing a diverse skill set, you can future-proof your video editing skills and stay ahead in the ever-evolving industry. If you have any questions or need further details on any of these strategies, feel free to ask!

AFTERWORD

As we reach the conclusion of *The Visual Maestro's Handbook: Mastering Modern Video Editing*, it's time to reflect on the journey we've undertaken together. From mastering the essentials and exploring advanced techniques to delving into the latest trends and innovations, this book has aimed to equip you with the knowledge and skills needed to excel in the ever-evolving world of video editing.

Throughout these chapters, we've covered a vast array of topics, each contributing to the multifaceted craft of video editing. By now, you should feel confident in your ability to craft compelling stories, enhance visuals, and produce high-quality content that captivates audiences. But remember, this is just the beginning. The world of video editing is dynamic, constantly offering new challenges and opportunities for growth.

A Journey of Lifelong Learning

Embracing the role of a visual maestro means committing to continuous learning and growth. Stay curious, experiment with new techniques, and never stop seeking inspiration. The skills you've gained from this book are valuable, but the real magic happens when you apply them with creativity and passion.

Embracing Innovation

Technology is advancing at an unprecedented pace, introducing tools and techniques that were once unimaginable. By staying informed about emerging trends like AI, VR, and cloud-based collaboration, you can remain at the forefront of the industry. Embrace these innovations, and don't be afraid to push the boundaries of what's possible.

Building a Community

The journey of a video editor is often collaborative. Building a strong network of peers, mentors, and collaborators can be incredibly rewarding. Share your knowledge, learn from others, and support fellow creators. Together, we can push the art of video editing to new heights.

A Note of Gratitude

A heartfelt thank you to all the readers who have embarked on this adventure with me. Your passion for storytelling and dedication to honing your craft are truly inspiring. I hope this book has been a valuable resource and will continue to serve as a guide in your future projects.

The Future

As you move forward, remember that every project is an opportunity to tell a story, evoke emotions, and make an impact. Whether you're creating content for social media, working on a personal passion project, or producing professional videos, your unique perspective and creativity are what make your work special.

Thank you for allowing me to be a part of your journey. Here's to many more stories, countless frames, and endless creativity. Stay inspired, stay passionate, and keep editing.

Happy editing,

Yatendra Kumar Singh 'Manuh

❖ ❖ ❖

www.ingramcontent.com/pod-product-compliance
Lightning Source LLC
LaVergne TN
LVHW022348060326
832902LV00022B/4325